Perpetual Spring

SINGAPORE'S

Gardens by the Bay

Koh Buck Song

Gardens by the Bay make up to the world's lineup of

Singapore's contribution premier public gardens.

Message 8

Foreword 10

1 Introduction
Making a Garden 12

2 Genesis
The First Seeds 26

3 The Conservatories
Into Other Worlds 54

4 The Supertrees
Green Giants, Vertical Gardens 114

5 Themed Gardens
Nature's Bounty 154

6 Lakes and Main Gardens
Clean Waters, Fragile Forest 178

7 A New Future of Perpetual Spring 216

Acknowledgements 230

Message

Singapore has long recognised the importance of a green environment to our wellbeing, peace of mind and sense of belonging. Nature is an integral part of our urban landscape. Green spaces such as the Botanic Gardens, neighbourhood parks, nature reserves, and Active, Beautiful and Clean Waters are fully integrated into our environment. Gardens by the Bay is the latest expression of our vision to transform Singapore into a City in a Garden.

With its strategic location and unique design, Gardens by the Bay lends a distinctive flair to the Marina Bay skyline. It is an outstanding leisure destination, which contributes to making Singapore a global city of distinction. Besides being an international icon, the Gardens must also be a focal point for the local community. I hope that as many people as possible enjoy Gardens by the Bay, whether to take a stroll, learn about plants and flowers, or participate in events. Community involvement is an important measure of its success.

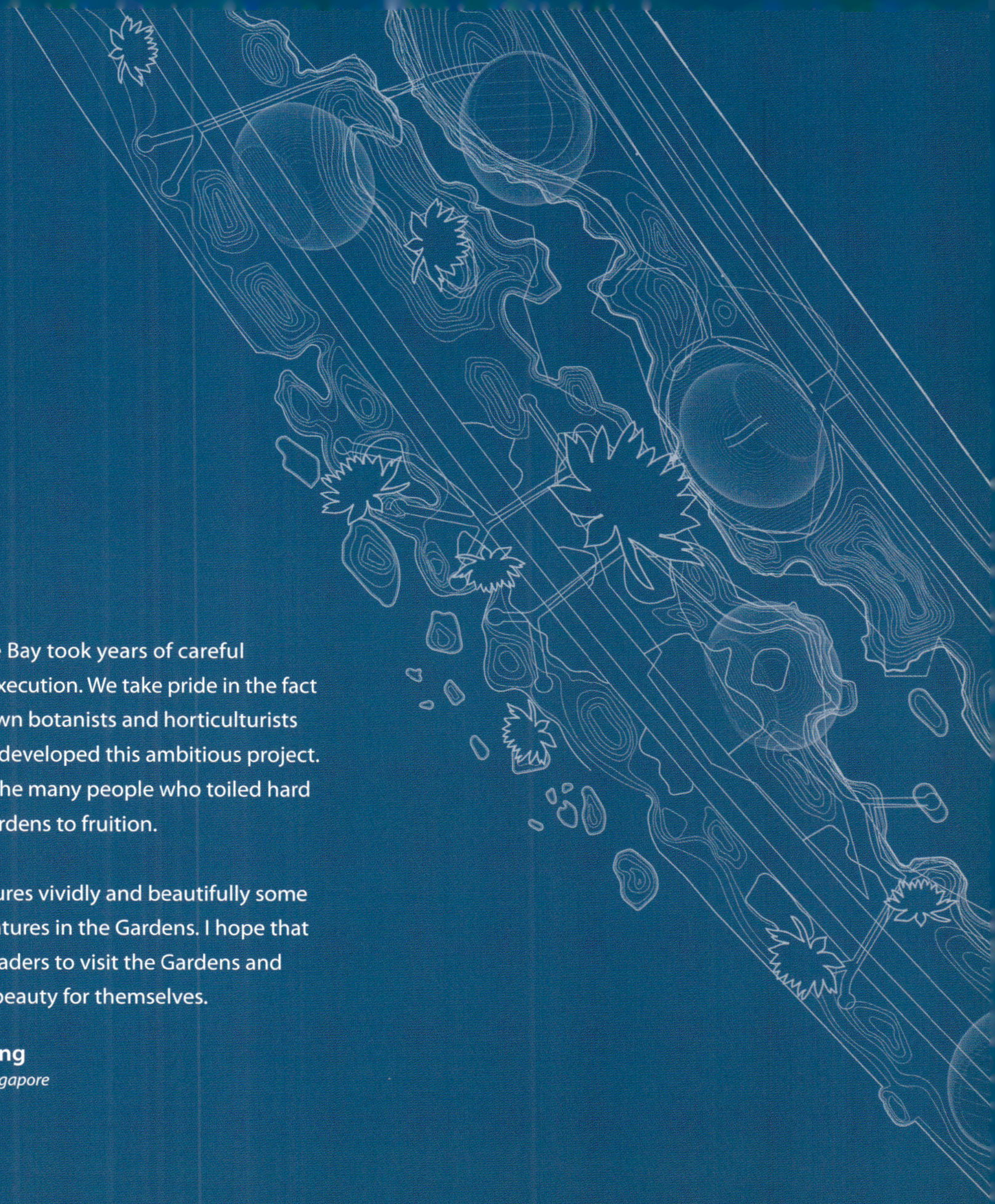

Gardens by the Bay took years of careful planning and execution. We take pride in the fact that our very own botanists and horticulturists conceived and developed this ambitious project. I congratulate the many people who toiled hard to bring the Gardens to fruition.

This book captures vividly and beautifully some of the many features in the Gardens. I hope that it will inspire readers to visit the Gardens and experience its beauty for themselves.

Lee Hsien Loong
Prime Minister of Singapore
28 June 2012

Foreword

The formation of Gardens by the Bay marks a milestone in the journey travelled by Singapore from Garden City to Garden Nationhood. Gardens by the Bay serves as the complementary bookend to the iconic Singapore Botanic Gardens, providing the horticultural anchor to the botanical aspirations of its organisational twin. The Singapore Botanic Gardens has established its credentials as a key international institution of tropical botany. The Gardens by the Bay takes pride in its genesis as the people's garden of Singapore, delighting the residential community here on the Equator in Southeast Asia with its celebration of the plant world.

The determinedly populist stance of the Gardens by the Bay fronts a decidedly serious agenda touching upon social, cultural, environmental and ultimately educational motives. Using interpretation of the Plant Kingdom in all its diversity as the vehicle of communication, Gardens by the Bay seeks to engage the Singapore community in its entirety on matters concerning citizenry integration, environmental sustainability, political cohesion and the bridging of the generational divide.

Such aspirations can only be achieved by first capturing the attention of the target audience — hence the creation of world-class, eye-catching, innovative and imaginative infrastructure with which to showcase and sustain an awesome array of plants from nearly every continent on earth. The Gardens by the Bay is unique in many ways, the most notable of which is that the conception and development of this groundbreaking project is led by a team of home-grown botanists and horticulturists, the plantsmen responsible for the greening of Singapore over the last three decades.

If a garden is indeed one of the highest forms of cultural attainment of a nation, then such an arrangement is most appropriate. The masterplan and architecture of Gardens by the Bay is predicated upon the needs of the plant material for the landscape, and upon the imperative of providing physical comfort to the people who visit or work on its premises. Aesthetic, economic, functional and educational considerations underlie all decisions, with sustainability of the Gardens and the general wellbeing of visitors providing the guiding principles. For example, the design of the two glass domes and the Supertrees of steel and concrete owe their forms and locations to adherence to the above parameters. Even manifestations of whimsy and eccentricity have passed through the pragmatic filters that inform the creation of this quintessential Singaporean product. The unequivocal focus is upon the engagement of the local population.

Once attention is captured by the infrastructure, the task is to sustain and retain interest of the public. This is the responsibility of the team set up to provide excellent interpretative programming and visitor services to keep Gardens by the Bay competitive as a recreational destination. The challenge is to sustain relevance, with the capacity to delight and surprise Singaporeans in the face of intense competition for that precious time allocated for relaxation, recreation and entertainment by a goal-driven people whose private space and time is under constant siege.

Ultimately, the future of Gardens by the Bay rests upon its acceptance by the people of Singapore as an essential amenity for their enjoyment of life here. They must be willing to embrace Gardens by the Bay with pride and the requisite sense of ownership that encompasses care and advocacy for its continual support and enhancement. This garden on the Equator is the latest evidence of a stewardship that prioritises the wellbeing of its people by a government with an indubitable reputation for efficiency and efficacy. A garden is a living entity. As with all living systems, adaptation and evolution are constant processes that shape growth and development. With time, the Gardens by the Bay will come to reflect more truly the nature of the people of Singapore to the world. Our hope is that the Gardens by the Bay will endure as Singapore's garden for all seasons, and for all time.

Dr Kiat W Tan
Chief Executive Officer, Gardens by the Bay

1 Introduction

Making a Garden

Gardening has been a most fascinating interface between Man and Nature since the beginning of time.

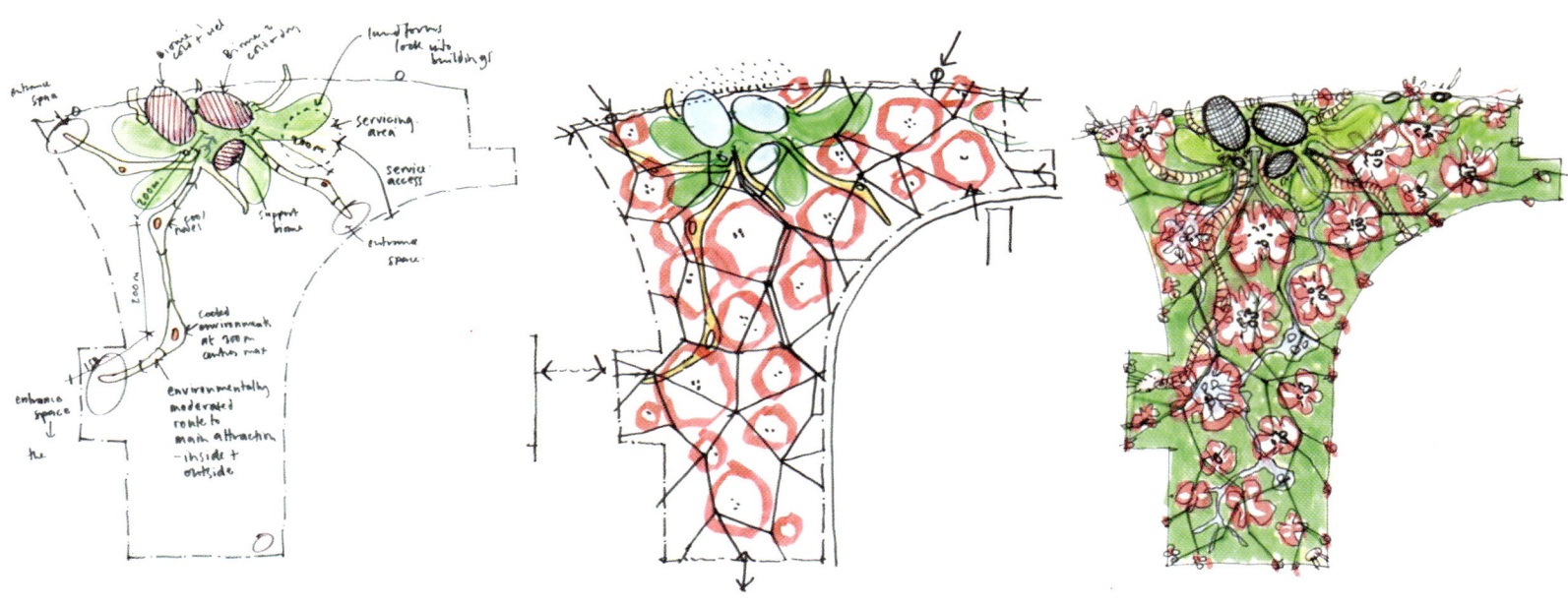

Gardening has been a most fascinating interface between Man and Nature since the beginning of time. The very act of making and managing a garden — every weed that is plucked, every seed pressed into earth — is to impose Man's will, to exert influence over shrubs and saplings, trees and thorns. The outcome, when well-done, can be nothing less than immensely fruitful, the pun fully intended. To add beauty and pleasure to life in this way can be nothing short of wonderful. Singapore's Gardens by the Bay offers this, and more.

In Singapore, the two activities of gardening and applying human ingenuity and endeavour are more central to the future than in most other places. Overcoming natural constraints has always been the only path to survival and success for this small nation with no natural resources except a strategic geographical location and any human talent it can marshal and motivate. As for greenery and plants, the Republic has always placed gardens very high on the national agenda.

The urgency and mission of Gardens by the Bay is to capture public attention, including that of the unconverted man in the street, with the sheer fascination of the plant kingdom, and to promote understanding and appreciation for the need to preserve and nurture the environment. On these two parameters, Gardens by the Bay is Singapore's newest and most ambitious offering to share with the world.

This set of public gardens will be spread across 101 hectares in three adjoining locations, right on the city centre waterfront and linked by bridges over Marina Bay. Whole new worlds of botanical wonder will be created in a manner — and on a scale — unprecedented in this part of the globe. The plants on show will present the best of Singaporean flora — specimens to be showcased in something as local as a Peranakan spice, or something more exotic, such as a botanical slice of South America.

The two glass conservatories of Gardens by the Bay — cocoons of wonder, and twin havens of cool-dry and cool-moist environments — will enable visitors to transcend and conquer time and space, to sense, smell and savour faraway realms from Madagascar to Mexico, to soak in springtime any day of the year. The two domes will allow visitors to traverse vast regions and be transported from Mediterranean to montane climates in a matter of minutes. The world will be a smaller place — for residents in Singapore to take a 'botanical' holiday whenever they wish, and for anyone anywhere to visit and see the world in one place. Singapore as an 'air-conditioned nation' will take on a whole new meaning. Perpetual spring will add a vital new dimension to this place of eternal summer.

Pages 16–17: Singapore's financial district is reflected in this pond at the former Marina City Park, at the site where Bay South Garden is today.

Gardens have always been central to Singapore's global positioning. Since the 1960s, this young nation, fully independent only from 1965, has cultivated its international reputation as a Garden City, a city-state in which gardens are pervasively included at the highest priority in all aspects of urban planning. Over the years, many international visitors have come to see this dimension for themselves. The first impression of one big, well-kept garden is maintained as a matter of daily ritual, right from the initial sights of the country as seen from the highway going into the city from Changi Airport — with the East Coast Parkway flanked by lush, spruced plantings and now leading up to the majestic first sight of Gardens by the Bay at the fringe of the Central Business District.

Much as the last five decades have affirmed the wisdom of adopting this model of greening a nation, true to form for Singapore, re-invention never rests, as the country all the time has its sights firmly trained on the distant horizon as it prepares for the future 24/7 and 365 days a year.

A new paradigm has been seeded since the early years of the 21st century, and the new model is that of a City in a Garden, an ingenious conceptual inversion, to have, instead, the whole country growing as one big garden in which urban centres are built fully integrated and immersed amidst all the greenery and flora. This much more holistic nurturing of Nature is the strategic backdrop against which Gardens by the Bay now ushers in a whole new era for a green Singapore.

The global gallery of top gardens welcomes its newest showpiece with the successful completion of the building of Gardens at Bay South, the main gardens of the Gardens by the Bay project. The other two gardens also fringe the water across Marina Bay and Marina Channel — Bay East across the Marina Barrage, and Bay Central near the Singapore Flyer. The three gardens are set to be the premier attractions of this kind in the tropics, as well as an iconic addition to the world's collection of the best public gardens. Anyone who wishes to tour the top gardens of the world would now add Gardens by the Bay to the must-visit list.

For Singapore, as Dr Kiat W Tan, director of the Gardens by the Bay project since its official inception in 2005, has said, the Gardens are an amenity for everyone in the country to enjoy for all time: "Gardens by the Bay will be perpetually accessible to all Singaporeans and their guests. Such public places will come to embody and signify the homeland for which duty, love, honour and sacrifice are due."

Almost seven years in the making, Gardens by the Bay is a labour of love. And this, from the very notion of setting aside such a prime piece of land in what is rather unusual a site — at the extended (and, again, man-made) land around the mouth of the Singapore River, and flanked by the futuristic urban structures of an expanded downtown. These shimmering glass skyscrapers, artistic creations of steel and concrete, also echo the essence of botanical aesthetics and sustainability in Gardens by the Bay, with their skyrise greenery of trees and shrubs on towering balconies and roof terraces.

The Marina Bay skyrise greenery example of extending the celebration of all that is green will also be reflected in the rest of Singapore as a City in a Garden, much as Gardens by the Bay aspires to inspire a similar cherishing elsewhere around the globe — through the Gardens' visitors — of the essential beauty of Nature and the efforts of Man to adapt and apply aspects of Nature to find a new balance. This will be Gardens by the Bay's gift to the world. This will be its enduring legacy.

Opposite: The masterplan design submitted by Grant Associates for the International Masterplan Design Competition held in 2006. *Pages 22–23:* Some visitors to Bay South Garden will recall happy times spent at the location previously, when it used to be the Marina City Park.

The dragonfly as IDEAL SYMBOL

As the official symbol for Gardens by the Bay, used in the Gardens' corporate logo, the dragonfly is almost perfect — and that is no overstatement.

Common Parasol (*Neurothemis fluctuans*) on which the Gardens by the Bay logo is based

The alignment of image with identity works even in relation to the very shape of the gardens. The three gardens of Gardens by the Bay together make up Singapore's contribution to the world's lineup of premier public gardens. Seen from the air in aerial plan view, the three plots of land spaced out across Marina Bay resemble, with a little stretch of the imagination, a seahorse or a dragonfly.

That the shape of the land-plots of Gardens by the Bay bears some slight resemblance to the shape of the main island of Japan also carries with it another dragonfly connection. Japanese legend has it that an emperor was bitten by a horsefly, which, in turn, was eaten by a dragonfly. The emperor honoured the dragonfly by naming what is now Japan, *Akitsushima*, which, during that time, translated to 'Isle of the Dragonfly'. Looked at more closely, the various characteristics of the dragonfly are also reflected in the key features of Gardens by the Bay.

Pre-dating dinosaurs, dragonflies claim a lineage and heritage that fit in very well with Gardens by the Bay in its own aspiration to capture and convey all that is best from the whole history of botanical evolution, from the most ancient species of surviving flora right up to the most modern and recent application of technology in presenting the beauty of Nature.

More than 450 species of dragonfly are known to exist, and the extent to which they are viewed with affection in some cultures is illustrated by the fact that, in Japan for example, there are different popular names for each of the 200 species found there. This profusion of names could be said to be natural to the Japanese psyche, as seen in more modern examples of nomenclatural proliferation, such as the cartoon characters of the series called Pokemon. But, nonetheless, it would be hard to dispute the observation that, typically, one would take so much trouble to compile such an extensive catalogue of terms only if they are ones of intense endearment.

Dragonflies have six legs like any other insect but, possibly because of the balance they have to maintain due to their unique body shape, they are incapable of walking, and instead move around mostly by flying. Indeed, scientists are known to study the body and aerodynamic mechanics of this marvellous insect for possible application to the improvement of aircraft design, especially for helicopters. This means that dragonflies are always in flight, reflecting the dynamism and — aptly — the 'helicopter' vision of the Gardens themselves in their aspiration to capture a global frame of reference.

As a predator of other less welcome insects such as flies and mosquitoes, the dragonfly is an integral part of the ecosystem of the water bodies it inhabits. This makes the dragonfly also an ambassador for sustainability, another key theme of Gardens by the Bay, in the way that the Gardens harness the natural resources of energy and water in the various features as seen at the Bay South Garden. By contrast to the insects it eats, dragonflies are incapable of stinging or biting, except for just a gentle pinch, and even then, usually only under extreme provocation. This gentleness also reaffirms the overwhelmingly positive perceptions of dragonflies in many human cultures.

Ancient folklore in Europe contains interpretations of the dragonfly usually laden with suspicion and distrust. But more benign readings prevail elsewhere. To the Native American Navajo tribe, the dragonfly is a symbol of pure water. That it is taken as an indicator of water cleanliness is quite appropriate given its elongated body, lending it something of a dip-stick appearance. And a metaphorical dip-stick it indeed is, for the Gardens' concerted focus on preserving water purity in its elaborate system to pump and channel fresh water into its lake system comprising a number of open water bodies, the main ones being the Dragonfly and Kingfisher Lakes.

In some other beliefs, dragonflies are a symbol of renewal after a time of great hardship. The Vietnamese observe dragonflies to interpret the weather, predicting rain when they fly at low levels. In some parts of the world, it is considered lucky to have a dragonfly land on you, even to the point of yielding seven years of good luck.

Finally, and most fundamentally, the cultural diversity of the meanings attached to dragonflies links to the core of what Gardens by the Bay can stand for. In drawing to one place some of the most fascinating luxuriance of flora and greenery from the farthest ends of Planet Earth, the Gardens are a supreme symbol of botanical cosmopolitanism — like the multi-layered cultural interpretations of the dragonfly itself.

2
Genesis
The First Seeds

Of the many aspects that make Singapore's Gardens by the Bay unique, the prominence of its location must top the list.

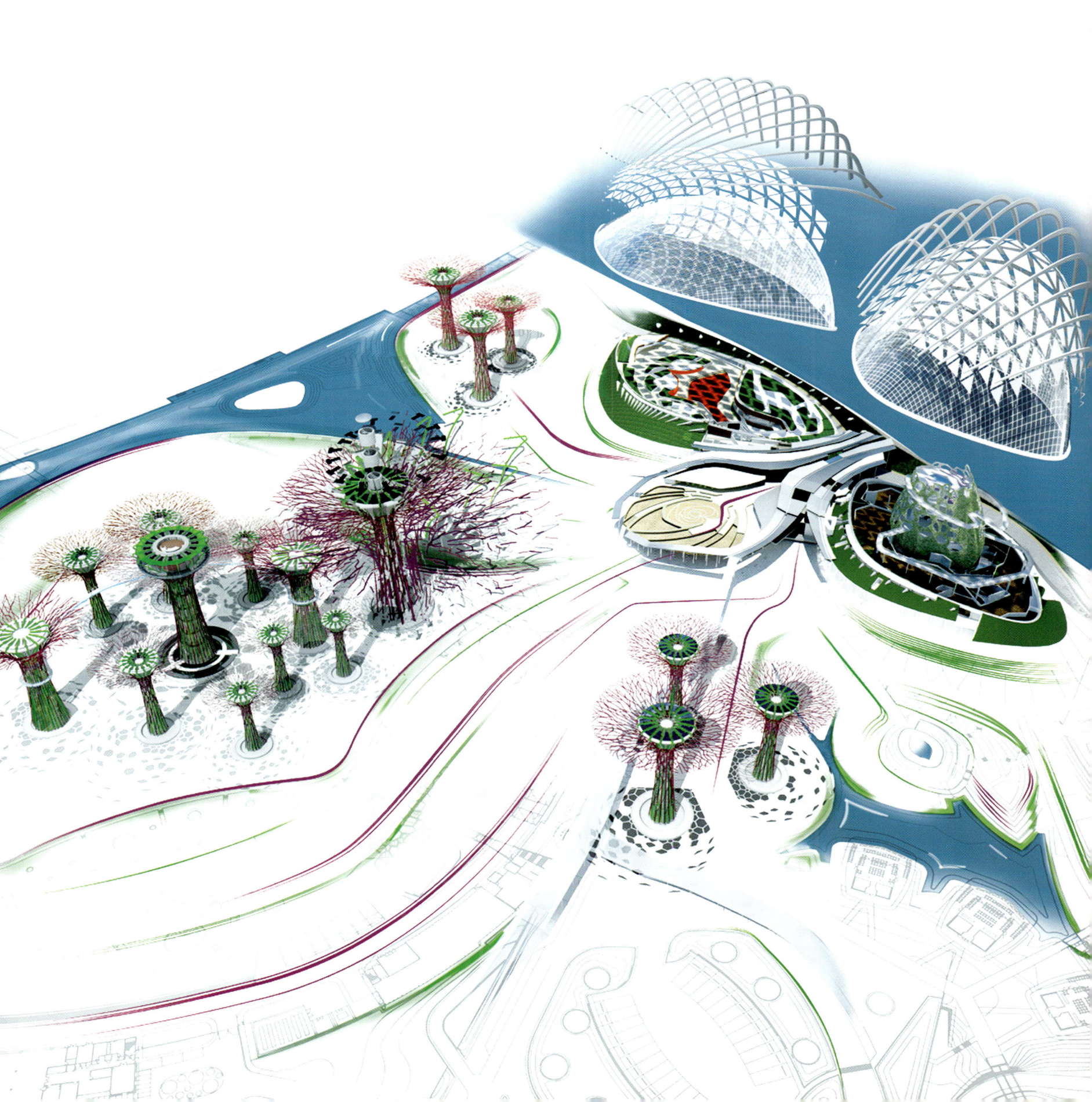

ELSEWHERE ON EARTH, THERE ARE MAJOR CITY PARKS THAT — LITERALLY AND GEOGRAPHICALLY — ARE AT THE HEARTBEAT OF THE CITY, SUCH AS NEW YORK'S CENTRAL PARK IN THE USA. BUT GARDENS BY THE BAY IS SOMETHING ELSE.

Elsewhere on Earth, there are major city parks that — literally and geographically — are at the heartbeat of the city, such as New York's Central Park in the USA. There are gardens within earshot of ocean waves, such as Perth's Kings Park and Botanic Garden in Australia. But Gardens by the Bay is something else. Placed not only in the very heart of Singapore's new downtown at Marina Bay, serene by the coastal waters stretching south towards the Indonesian archipelago visible to the naked eye, these gardens are also right on the national shorefront, at the mouth of the Singapore River, immersed in the sparkling Marina Channel and Marina Reservoir. A comelier confluence of water, wind and wonder is hard to imagine.

To mix a metaphor, Singapore is an old hand at having green fingers. Gardens have been huge on the national agenda since the 1960s. Recent data has put some hard numbers on this differentiating facet of soft infrastructure. From 1986 to 2007, when Singapore's population increased by about 80 per cent, the island's green cover expanded from 35.7 per cent to 46.5 per cent. By 2008, 9 per cent of the country's 700 square kilometres of landmass had been committed to parks and nature reserves, along with 103 kilometres of park connectors linking up beautiful canals and rivers to turn the whole island into a realisation of its new vision — to be a City in a Garden.

For decades already internationally renowned as a Garden City, Singapore's new vision for a new chapter — to become a City in a Garden — is an ingenious inversion of terms for a bright new proposition. From being a city that prioritises sustaining gardens in key places, the whole country is now becoming one big garden. The growth of the city is thus placed not on top of, but within, that larger context — now it is garden first, then city, not the other way around as it had been for much of the first 30 years of independence. This crucial paradigm shift in urban planning is the foundation upon which Gardens by the Bay establishes its location — an approach and, indeed, philosophy, that sees the choicest real estate, including 8.1 kilometres of waterfront, allocated to gardens instead of commercial development.

The stage is now set to showcase the latest of Singapore's remarkable investments in greenery in yet another enterprise of fruitful promise — seeking after the best presentation of Nature through human ingenuity. In this horticultural fantasia, pervasive greenery is linked and integrated with the urban fabric, creating an intense and seamless experience that extends from streetscapes to sky gardens.

> FROM BEING A CITY THAT PRIORITISES SUSTAINING GARDENS IN KEY PLACES, THE WHOLE COUNTRY IS NOW BECOMING ONE BIG GARDEN ... NOW IT IS GARDEN FIRST, THEN CITY.

Dr Kiat W Tan, Chief Executive Officer of Gardens by the Bay, knows, perhaps better than anyone else, what a gem has been secured with the Gardens' locational pre-eminence: "The site itself is spectacular, because all along the Marina Channel we have unimpeded views," he says.

And the considerations extend far beyond the aesthetic. The two cooled conservatories were sited specifically on the water's edge, so that the sun would cast far fewer shadows in an east-west orientation from nearby buildings and trees, or from the domes' own internal structures. This is to usher in maximum light — crucial to triggering flowering. And this is the vital act of prompting life-force inside the domes, which have been dubbed 'glass arks' by the media for the domes' contribution to profiling the key messages of sustainability.

["THE SITE ITSELF IS SPECTACULAR, BECAUSE ALL ALONG THE MARINA CHANNEL WE HAVE UNIMPEDED VIEWS."

Occupying close to two hectares of ground footprint under glass, the operation of the conservatories would have to be just as, if not more, economical and efficient than any office buildings in the city. And here is where human ingenuity comes in to sustain these new wonders.

If there are observers — no doubt, including some purists — who would wish that the greenery all over Singapore were more 'natural', it would help to see that the intervention of Man, as it were, in fact goes back a much longer way. Dr Tan notes that after Sir Stamford Raffles founded modern Singapore for the then British Empire in 1819, much of the original vegetation on the island was progressively cleared for urban development. "So in a way," he says, "Nature in Singapore had to be reinstated" even from those days, let alone later on. Early on from the beginning, then, the starting point in the consideration of the place of gardens was that a garden is, and always will be, to some extent a man-made artifice, and Singapore was all along well-placed for gardens to be recreated

and renewed. Noting that today's mantra in Singapore for conserving Nature and the environment is "reduce, reuse, recycle", he says, "I would add three more Rs to that. I would say: renew, reclaim and realise."

The three additional Rs apply well to Gardens by the Bay. Singapore itself is a 'renewed' country, in greenery terms, with about 30 per cent of land already reclaimed from the sea, and with more sand being pumped into the water almost all the time at some spot in the country. Now, Gardens by the Bay stands to realise the new priorities of the City in a Garden. Dr Tan sees another dimension to this work of restoration — to reclaim the bio-turf that used to be in Singapore, to renew its very biodiversity itself. In so doing, Dr Tan gives new meaning to the old expression 'son of the soil'. Gardens by the Bay will be a gardens built from scratch, springing up out of waste soil. Its fundamental elements will be water, energy and biodiversity.

Of all the hurdles to overcome, Dr Tan is very clear which ones matter most: "The most challenging, of course, is to get approval for the funding in a nation that is pragmatic to a fault. So you must imagine how convincing we must be, that we are being very practical when we do this." To persuade the Cabinet to back his ambitious plans, the support of key ministers was crucial, especially then Minister Mentor Lee Kuan Yew, for whom gardens had always been vital in the national economic strategy since the 1960s, and then National Development Minister Mah Bow Tan, under whose charge the City in a Garden vision was formulated and assumed its first form.

The second key challenge — the wider backing for the funding — has been solved with time, Dr Tan believes. "As Singapore evolved as a Garden City and we are having the support of the Government and the people for such places, it's obvious we now need green lungs more than ever. So, as for the concept of having a future central park in this part of the world surrounded by high-rises, Central Park has proven its value in New York, Hyde Park and Kensington Park in London. Singapore will have its Gardens by the Bay. And this will be a garden — about the size of Hyde Park — that has a body of water at its heart. So it will create that impression of a tropical dream garden that will delight the senses."

It is hard to miss the feeling of good fortune in Dr Tan's appreciation of the happy circumstances in which Gardens by the Bay has come into being. "Being fortunate in timing is something you can't plan. But Singapore is at a time of good economic growth and it has accumulated sufficient resources for us to indulge in this, what would have been a luxury in the past that we could not afford. And we would still not be able to afford it if it had not gone beyond luxury, to a need to have."

Pages 32–33: Part of the site where Bay East Garden will be built, across the Marina Channel from Bay South Garden. This particular plot was prepared for the water sports events of the inaugural Youth Olympic Games in Singapore in 2010.

Just as the Gardens by the Bay's highlight features of the two cooled conservatories had their prototype glasshouses at HortPark off Alexandra Road, Gardens by the Bay itself as a project had an early precursor that dates back to 1989.

That was the year that Dr Tan first mooted the idea of building a cooled conservatory in Singapore. This, of course, was a visionary botanist's dream in the tropics — to construct the climatic opposite of the familiar greenhouse in temperate climates, this time cool instead of warm, with temperatures cooled below the sweltering heat outdoors, so that an awesome parallel universe would become possible, that plants of another, much cooler world could come to survive and reside this close to the Equator.

Now, Gardens by the Bay opens up another new universe of Nature — realms of perpetual spring amidst scorching summer, and cocoons of other continents. And so, within 30 minutes from Singapore's city centre one can be immersed in the various environments of a beach, Mediterranean scrub, cloud forest or wetland. And any purist who is uncomfortable with artifice would do well to see that, while the hard exoskeleton of Gardens by the Bay may be man-made, its insides are nothing but soft and natural. And there is something truly precious about being able to see, smell, touch and feel botanical fragments of distant lands and microclimates right here in Singapore.

The first concept was somewhat less ambitious. An architect no less distinguished than the Sri Lankan Geoffrey Bawa (1919–2003) was commissioned by the then Singapore Tourist Promotion Board in 1989 to start to realise the dream of a significant coolhouse. What emerged from Bawa's drawing board was a design of pyramidal structure, a model of which was housed at the Gardens by the Bay's development site office in Marina South

throughout the construction of the Gardens between 2006 and 2011. Bawa's concept was problematic from the start, attracting detractors for, among other things, evoking the design controversies surrounding the pyramidal Louvre Museum in Paris, France, when the latter was unveiled in 1989. There were also those who were not convinced that Bawa's pyramids would be energy-efficient enough. And so, the proposal was shelved, a phoenix to rise another day, in a more welcoming environment.

Despite this, there was an interim realisation of this idea, as Dr Tan persevered with it and a smaller coolhouse with a tropical montane forest environment — one-tenth the original scale — was built eventually at the Singapore Botanic Gardens in 2004. This experimentation would come to enhance the National Orchid Garden's display and add to the understanding of the related technology. But it was not until Gardens by the Bay that the original dream would reach fruition in modified form, and much more substantially than it was imaginable at first.

And so, fast forward to the year 2003–04, when the whole country was caught up in wanting to reinvent Singapore into a global city of distinction. And here, there is perhaps an interesting parallel between a new motivation in the world of Man and of Nature. Just as the nation's perennial drive to boost economic competitiveness had now found a new edge in the global sourcing of highly mobile human capital, there was fresh occasion to create a garden that would be man-made but would be no less able to woo migratory birds to visit, forage and nest. By extension, what the feathered migrants enjoy would lift the quality of life, and so also draw migrants of the unfeathered kind.

> FROM THE START, GARDENS BY THE BAY WAS MEANT TO CLAIM ITS PLACE AMONG THE LEADING PUBLIC GARDENS OF THE WORLD.

The Urban Redevelopment Authority, through former Chief Planner Koh Wen Jin, was ready to allocate this swathe of greenery to add to the green matrix of the whole island. It was great timing, also, for what had been for some time a growing urge to do something to relieve the swelling visitor pressure on the Singapore Botanic Gardens, which had been hosting some three million visitors a year. A challenge was brewing in terms of balancing between catering to recreation as well as horticulture and botanical research.

Another new location would help, another national garden. Hence, a Cabinet paper was put up for a second botanic gardens, what Kenneth Er, Assistant CEO of National Parks Board and Chief Operating Officer of Gardens by the Bay, calls the 'east of Eden' project. The Eden referred to was not the biblical botanical haven, but the Eden Project in Cornwall, England, then the world's most innovative botanical attraction. Part of the original idea was to have one garden for botanical research and development and the other garden for horticulture. But this was to change crucially, so much so that some effort was spent for a while to stop people from referring to Gardens by the Bay as a second botanic gardens, because its remit had taken a different direction.

At about that time, there was another Cabinet paper that became part of the germination of Gardens by the Bay. This paper argued for the establishment of a Singapore Garden Festival, a flower and garden show that would one day rank alongside other top shows on the international calendar such as the Chelsea Flower Show in London, England. Among other things, it was envisaged that a Singapore Garden Festival would help galvanise the country behind the new City in a Garden vision. Originally named the Singapore Tropical Garden Show, the concept was welcomed as a very appealing idea that first needed a venue. The Marina City Park, then being eyed for the country's possible second botanic gardens, could serve this purpose as well. This became an added push for the go-ahead for Gardens by the Bay, a direction supported by then Permanent Secretary of the Ministry of National Development, Tan Tee How. There was a need to make the business case for Gardens by the Bay, before a marker for the project could be plotted into such a choice sliver of prime land. The Government also had to be convinced that the Gardens was feasible from other standpoints, such as the energy point of view.

With the green light signalled for this greenest of projects, its true flowering blossomed far beyond its first seeds. The URA's Koh Wen Jin and its former Chief Executive Officer, Cheong-Chua Koon Hean, scanned the whole Marina Bay area and asked, why not be bolder, why

not go for a larger footprint for Gardens by the Bay? Dr Tan had wanted only a space no smaller than the Singapore Botanic Gardens, which the Marina South site was at 54 hectares (the exact dimension was selected for its auspicious meaning — 'never die' — in the Chinese dialect of Cantonese). This site was smaller than the first-proposed figure of 80 hectares, but the whole final total came to be easily surpassed as the URA offered two other plots — Bay East at 32 hectares and Bay Central at 15 hectares.

Guided by the abiding metaphor of a necklace of attractions strung across the Bay, the move to connect the three plots across the Marina Channel waters would complete the green link and embrace the Marina Reservoir. Importantly, too, it would secure the two additional strips of land for government ownership, and hence, for public use in perpetuity as part of the nation's public landbank. This notion was something very close to Dr Tan's heart. To him, a national garden had to have the buy-in and support of the home crowd. And for this to happen, as he saw it, this sentiment must prevail: "I should feel that I own the best parts of Singapore and enjoy access to the best parts of the country." And access should apply in every sense, including free entry. This was why he had always fought, over the years, for the Botanic Gardens to have no admission charges except for the National Orchid Garden. This model will operate at Gardens by the Bay as well, with only the conservatories and aerial walkway levying entrance fees.

From the start, Gardens by the Bay was meant to claim its place among the leading public gardens of the world. To get a sense of where the international standards and best practices were at, a March 2005 study trip led by Mr Mah took a delegation to Cornwall (Eden Project), New York (Central Park, New York Botanical Garden, Brooklyn Botanic Garden), Philadelphia (Longwood Gardens), Chicago (Millennium Park), Sarasota (Marie Selby Botanical Gardens), Atlanta (Atlanta Botanical Garden) and Miami (Fairchild Tropical Botanic Garden, The Kampong).

And to ensure that Gardens by the Bay was benchmarked against the world's best, an International Advisory Panel of the Singapore Botanic Gardens in June 2005 was asked to give advice on the roles and goals of the new Gardens. The panel included illustrious names such as Sir Peter Crane, Director of Kew Gardens in London, England; Dr Michael Maunder, Director of Fairchild Tropical Botanic Garden in Miami, Florida, USA; Dr James Folsom, Director of Huntington Botanical Gardens in San Marino, California, USA; and Dr Weerachai Nanakorn, Director of Queen Sirikit Botanic Garden in Chiangmai, Thailand. Their view was that Gardens by the Bay should, among other things, focus on aesthetics and experience, seek to nurture biodiversity, showcase the link between cultural diversity and plants in areas such as trade, and promote sustainability. Costings were compared with those of the Eden Project in England and Millennium Park in Chicago, Illinois, USA.

Pages 38–39 and opposite: Images of the old Marina City Park.

With a good sense of what Gardens by the Bay could aspire to become, an international masterplan competition was launched in 2006 to allow for the most imaginative and ambitious concepts to surface.

To Dr Tan, the good response to the global search for the best ideas bore testimony to how strong a draw Gardens by the Bay was. He recalled that he was astounded by the high levels of participation and professionalism in the 70 entries by 170 firms from 24 countries. The firms shortlisted included Alsop Design (UK), EDAW Australia, Field Operations (USA), Riken Yamamoto & Field Shop (Japan) and WIN Landscape Planning & Design (Japan). Some were landscape-driven, others architecture-driven, yet others hybrid models. Overall, they sought to make nature and architecture combine in new ways to produce new cultural landscapes. Gardens by the Bay would not just consume resources, but would also contain the capacity to produce new knowledge.

A high-powered 11-member jury panel — including renowned architects Fumihiko Maki of Japan and Peter Walker of the USA, and Dr James Folsom, Director of the Huntington Botanical Gardens in San Marino — eventually selected the winner. It decided to give two awards to the teams led by Andrew Grant (for Bay South) and Kathryn Gustafson (Bay East), with Bay Central kept for later development by homegrown designers. The two winning designs were "as different as night and day, and yin and yang". There was strategic value to having two winners instead of one, as the appeal of the two concepts straddled the generational divide. Dr Tan revealed that the Cabinet was evenly split in its response to the designs, with the younger ministers generally taking more to Grant's relatively funkier design, while the older ones preferred Gustafson's with its elegant coastal curves to maximise the view of the Central Business District.

Opposite site and this page: Grant Associates' winning submission for the 2006 International Masterplan Design Competition.
Above: Masterplan design of Gardens by the Bay submitted by Gustafson Porter.

[WITH GARDENS BY THE BAY AT THE HEART OF SINGAPORE'S NEW DOWNTOWN COMES THE MAKING OF AN IMPORTANT NEW CIVIC PLACE.

Dr Tan — who had been on URA competition boards and had worked on a Garden City project in Dubai — had briefed the designers to take into account Singapore's unique geography, history and phyto-geography. Grant at first took Singapore's history very literally, working politically symbolic elements such as the lion and the tiger into the design, but this was refined upon further development of the concept. Gardens by the Bay opted to go with his core plan with only minimal changes. For the backup number-crunching, a study by real estate developer Edmund Tie and accounting firm Ernst & Young was done for the Ministry of Finance. The timing of the project was good, as the marketing potential for the neighbouring Marina Bay Sands integrated resort had just been demonstrated. The vision of a garden lining the water, with the city springing forth behind, would present a perfect view of a leading tropical island nation with top gardens. This would go a long way to soften the 'hard persona' of Singapore. As a people's garden, Gardens by the Bay would also help anchor Singaporeans to the country. As Dr Tan said: "The beautiful memories and visions that people develop must include beauty and substance."

The unique features of the plot had their pros and cons. While reclaimed land allowed for unencumbered development, it also meant that key infrastructural features were not visible as they were all underground, including drains, sewers and canals. Only the last layer — the 'living skin' — could be seen. On this surface, Dr Tan has great plans. The displays at the Gardens, he says, will "use plants in ways people have never seen before".

Singapore is very well-placed, in a region blessed with not only the longest growing season in the world but also one of the wealthiest regions for biodiversity with neighbouring Borneo and Malaysia. The options for education and satisfying intellectual curiosity at the Gardens are immense, and so too, the opportunity to be a forum in Singapore for partnership with countries in the region with wonderful resources.

With Gardens by the Bay at the heart of Singapore's new downtown comes the making of an important new civic place. As then Minister for National Development Mah Bow Tan said in a *FuturArc* magazine interview (Volume 9, second quarter 2008): "We are not Dubai; we won't say to an architect, 'money is no object'. This is the budget and this is what you have to design. Within that budget, give us a building, a project that works. Make sure that it is easy to maintain but at the same time look at the form." Mr Mah calls Marina Bay Singapore's 'water Padang': "It is really the new Padang — a civic space — but in place of grass, there's water. A prominent architect once said it is like St Mark's Square in Venice." Major public developments in Singapore have always been a combination of form, function and finance. As Gardens by the Bay is unveiled, a spectacular new equation awaits.

[**A PEOPLE'S GARDEN: "THE BEAUTIFUL MEMORIES AND VISIONS THAT PEOPLE DEVELOP MUST INCLUDE BEAUTY AND SUBSTANCE."**

The design of Gardens by the Bay

For the Bay South Garden, Grant Associates UK landscape masterplanners and architects took the design lead. They were supported by collaborators Wilkinson Eyre (UK, architects), Atelier One (UK, design and structural engineers), Atelier Ten (UK, mechanical and electrical engineers), Meinhardt Infrastructure (civil and structural engineers) and Davis Langdon & Seah Singapore (quantity surveyors).

As Andew Grant understood it, the overall brief to the Gardens by the Bay designers was to "create a world-class garden that would be a leading tourist attraction. The ambition is to create the best tropical garden in the world — an outdoor space, landscape and green environment for locals and tourists to enjoy outdoor recreation." And this would be done in a totally new way. As Grant said: "Conceptually, I don't think there's anything like it anywhere, particularly in the tropics." Dramatic and extraordinary plant species, such as baobabs, are put together in groundbreaking ways. Vertical planting systems will add height, and sophisticated interpretations depth. And as if that were not enough, there is one more key element. "The unique thing here is interactivity."

Grant sees something else unique. "The incredibly diverse cultural mix here… is quite special and different. I don't think I've been anywhere else where it's so intrinsically part of the place. It's an amazing diversity." His multifaceted design will seek to capture that complexity. "Gardens by the Bay tries to create a space which conceptualises what Singapore is trying to be about, which is quite different than just making a green space. We're making a piece of space which represents what we think Singapore is about."

Into this design framework, Grant fitted in other aspects of the gardens to tackle a few 'happy problems'. One of these was to address a comment about Singapore that is common among visitors who come to see the Garden City and say that it is mostly green. To go one better, at Gardens by the Bay, the emphasis will be on colour — colourful foliage and very floriferous varieties of plants. This will be a garden of flowers and leaves of many hues. This injection of colour is already happening all over the rest of Singapore, from streetscape to skyrise.

Grant says his design offers a powerful and compelling mix of what he calls "Singapore ingredients":
- a climate that allows vigorous plant growth and vitality;
- commitment to innovation in both technological and intellectual progress;
- cosmopolitan culture;
- passion for progress;
- demand for improved quality of life, living and working environments; and the
- wish to fully engage with sustainable development and global environmental challenges.

As with so many other facets of Singapore, size would not be allowed to be a limitation. Some of the most important and famous gardens in the world, such as Ryoanji Garden in Kyoto, Japan, are less than one hectare in size. The main inspiration would be the Eden Project in Cornwall, England. For the festival aspect, precedents were sought from among possibilities including the Chaumont Garden Festival in France, Floriade in Holland and the Bundesgarten of Germany.

As Grant saw it, Gardens by the Bay would need "the magic of distinctiveness, strangeness, beauty and contrast". This overall aim was pursued by shaping the Gardens in terms of six aspects:
- as a valued resource by every resident of Singapore;
- as a physical, sensory and spatial expression unlike anything seen or yet imagined in the world;
- to stay true to a total examination and expression of the future relationship between people and plants, culture and the natural world;
- to become a world-renowned attraction and destination;
- to apply the most exemplary approaches to environmental sustainability and education; and
- as an exemplar of integrated open space planning and management, linking horticulture with living, recreation, science, art and culture, digital information and media, retail and commerce, food, leisure and education.

In Grant Associates' masterplan report, the Gardens were seen as "a landscape whose united beauty, magnificence and uniqueness will convey a perfect expression of Singapore". Fittingly for Singapore — the meaning of the gardens was intertwined very closely with that of the entire nation. "Rarely, if ever, can a landscape project have had such a profile and be linked so directly and intrinsically to the future identity and success of a country."

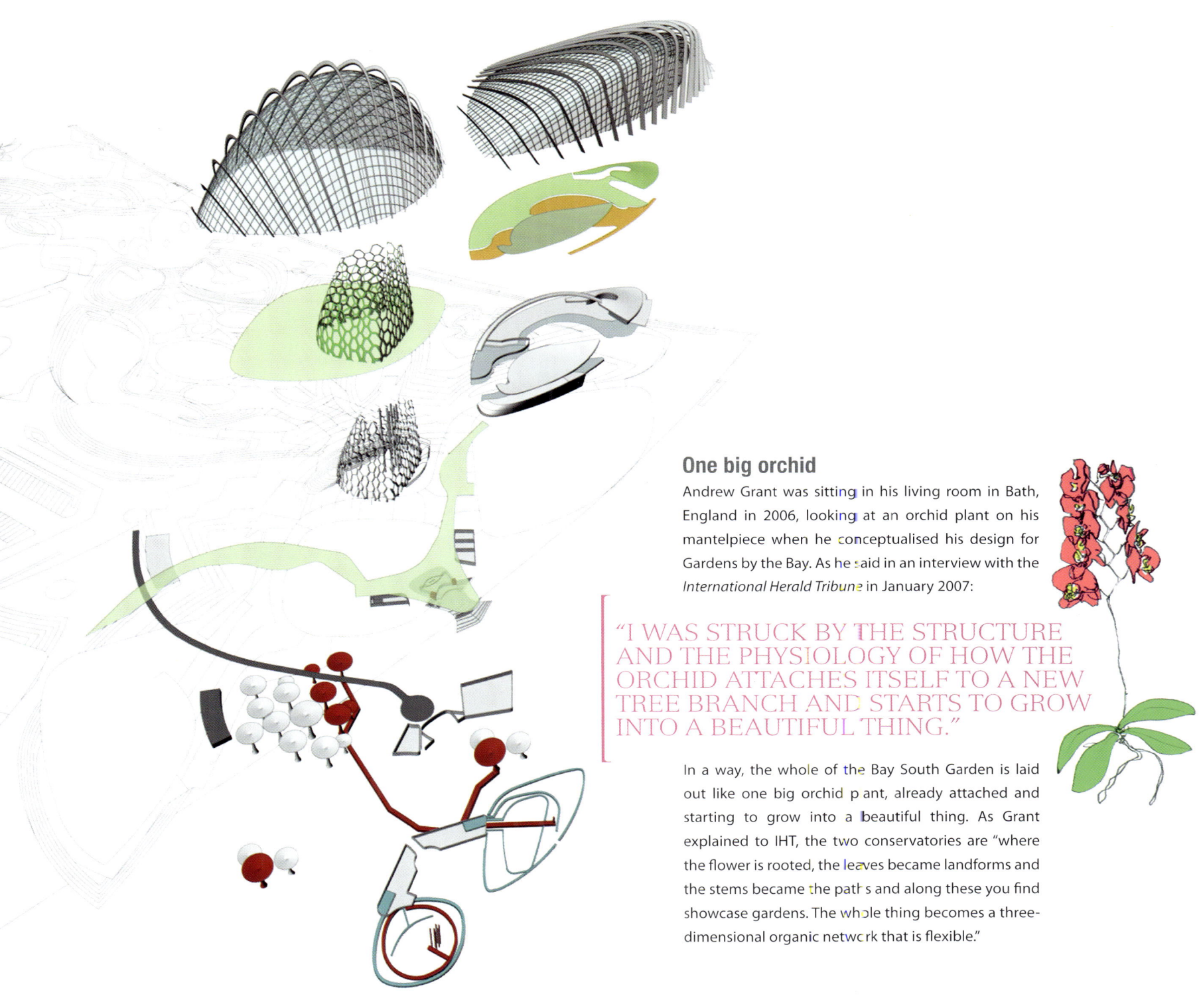

One big orchid

Andrew Grant was sitting in his living room in Bath, England in 2006, looking at an orchid plant on his mantelpiece when he conceptualised his design for Gardens by the Bay. As he said in an interview with the *International Herald Tribune* in January 2007:

> "I WAS STRUCK BY THE STRUCTURE AND THE PHYSIOLOGY OF HOW THE ORCHID ATTACHES ITSELF TO A NEW TREE BRANCH AND STARTS TO GROW INTO A BEAUTIFUL THING."

In a way, the whole of the Bay South Garden is laid out like one big orchid plant, already attached and starting to grow into a beautiful thing. As Grant explained to IHT, the two conservatories are "where the flower is rooted, the leaves became landforms and the stems became the paths and along these you find showcase gardens. The whole thing becomes a three-dimensional organic network that is flexible."

Reclaiming Eden:
GARDENS in THE BAY

In some senses, the Gardens by the Bay are gardens *in* the bay.

The Gardens at Bay South is built into land that was gradually reclaimed from the sea over 30 years. Land in the area sits on marine clay, which is soft and settles quickly, and over the years, the ground would also have subsided a bit. These factors pose issues with stability and make it more difficult for strong foundations to be built. The solution was two-fold — soil improvement and piling.

Soil improvement is a process in which soil is treated to help it to settle well and speed up earth consolidation. This was done using the vertical drain system. Strips of membrane — essentially strips of fabric — were installed some 30 metres deep into the ground and at 1 to 2 metres apart; the closer the interval, the faster the settlement. Earth loads and gravel were then piled onto the soil where the mounds and landforms were built, as high as 9 metres above ground. The weight of the load pushes the soil down, forcing water beneath the marine clay to travel up the strips of fabric, which act like tubes to drain out the water. In some places, the drop in the ground level as a result of the enhanced soil subsidence was as much as 3 metres. This process

of soil improvement for the entire Gardens site took between six to nine months to complete. As Dr Kiat W Tan, CEO of Gardens by the Bay, described it: "So, we're piling up earth on top to squeeze the water out. And eventually to create a little bit of rolling terrain."

However, not all areas required soil improvement, such as footpaths, which need not bear heavy loads. For areas where heavy specific structures were to be built, for instance the conservatories and Supertrees and where drains were to be laid, the alternative piling method was applied.

In this second method, piles were bored right through the soft marine clay to the good solid earth beneath it. In some places, the piles go as deep down as 50 metres. Several piles are held together by a pile cap, which is a cast of concrete block that 'caps' the piles and holds them together. Pile caps are vital to the foundation of a building. They distribute the weight of the building's columns and are designed to take in movement at the surface, while maintaining a firm and strong foundation underneath. When the building on the surface moves, for instance, because of strong winds (which are common in a tropical monsoon country like Singapore), the force of the movement is evenly transferred to the piles underneath, which are rooted deeply and firmly in the ground.

The challenge for the engineers was to determine which areas in the site to apply soil improvement and which areas to put in piling and foundations. This is because it is neither necessary nor desirable to put traditional building foundations under the whole Gardens; it is far better to let the earth do its natural thing.

Aside from these technical challenges, building on reclaimed land has other issues. Dealing with marine clay makes piling more expensive and adds to the overall cost. Giant boulders embedded in the soil had to be removed. Furthermore, the salt content of sea sand had dissipated from years of percolated rain which was a good thing, but this meant that there was also very little topsoil. New topsoil was created from a mixture of biowaste from the Gardens and sand. This recycling and renewal process is another aspect of sustainability, and another mark of man's mastery over the elements of Nature.

In the process of surcharging water from the reclaimed land, there was one incident that was initially unsettling, in more ways than one. About a week before the first groundbreaking ceremony in November 2007, Kenneth Er, Chief Operating Officer, and Ng Boon Gee, Assistant Director (Gardens Operations), were inspecting a mound that was originally meant to stand just southeast of the Cloud Forest conservatory. They were surprised to hear the hoardings around the area being rattled, until they realised that the mound they were standing on had started to collapse. The ground had subsided faster than anticipated, and the two men managed to leave the area in time. The spot was near the water's edge, and with the additional earth, the shoreline became extended outwards. What could have been a disaster had brought some unexpected positives. The area where the landslip happened is now a pocket of wetland that acts as a natural filter for the water from the Marina Channel, and also attracts bird and insect life. The spillover of soil into the Marina Reservoir also adds another aspect of how these are, in some ways, 'gardens *in* the bay'.

3
The Conservatories

Into Other Worlds

One encases a mountain, the other a valley. The pair of imposing structures cannot but stimulate the imagination.

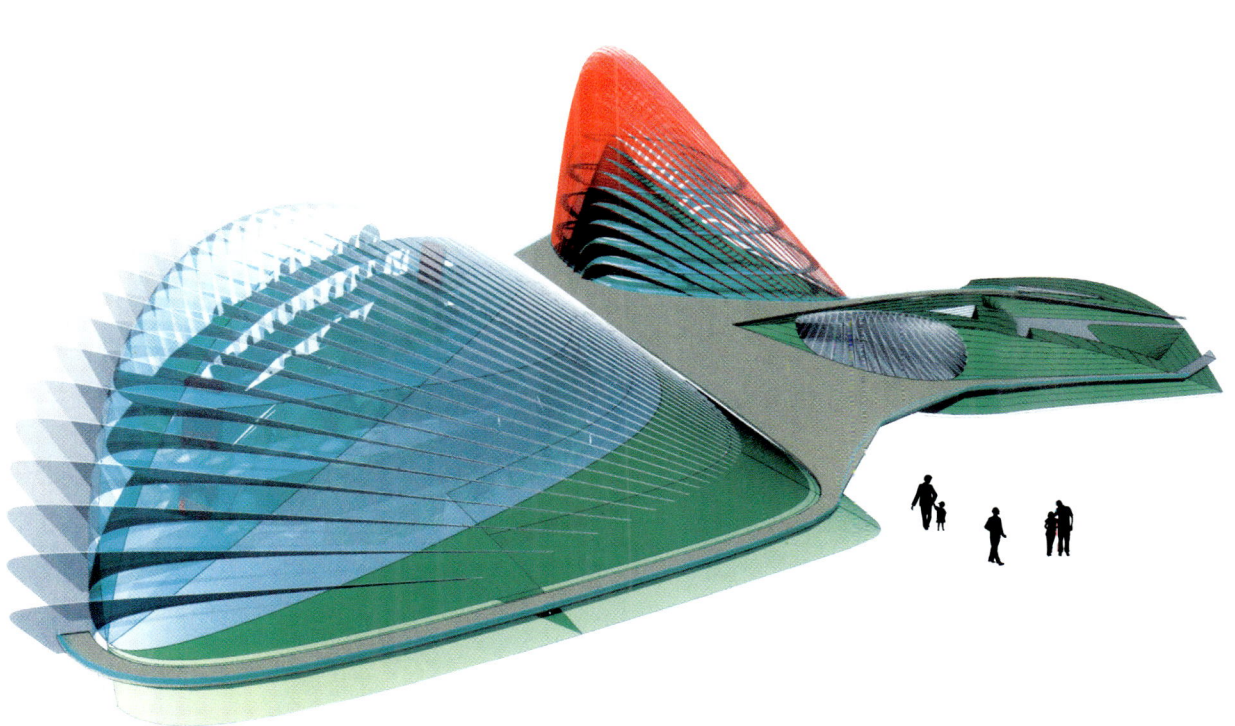

> THE TWO GLASSHOUSES ARE THE EQUATORIAL OPPOSITES OF TEMPERATE GREENHOUSES, COOL INSTEAD OF WARM INSIDE.

They rise imposingly when seen by road from the arched Benjamin Sheares Bridge on the East Coast Parkway, as one arrives at the city from the east, or by sea on a passing vessel from the south, or from a nearby tall building to the north or west, as more skyscrapers emerge in time at the new downtown around the Marina Bay Financial Centre. Majestic by day, mesmeric by night, these cooled conservatories house a wonderland within — two gigantic glass globes that transport visitors into two realms of botanical universe that are new to this part of the world.

The twin biomes are the highlights of Gardens by the Bay on several fronts. Visually, they

draw the eye irresistibly as much with their commanding presence as with their charismatic proportions. In height, they wrest the summit for bearing one of the two highest points of the entire complex along with the tallest Supertree. The biomes encapsulate crucial botanical significance with global environmental challenge, in what they display and depict. The domes form a troika among the Gardens' sights, together with the Supertrees, clusters of 18 giant concrete trees supporting vertical plantings.

The two glasshouses are the equatorial opposites of temperate greenhouses, cool instead of warm inside, and requiring to repel rather than retain heat. The simulated natural habitats within the two biomes — one cool-dry, the other cool-moist — replicate landscapes including some that are from far away, enabling the visitor to be spirited off to a distant new universe, to transport a Singaporean whether from Mountbatten or Marsiling, or a tourist from Macau or Madrid, into a magical Mediterranean or tropical montane forest, immersing explorers in the ambience of diverse botanical worlds. Both domes will house some 1,000 species of plants from every continent except Antarctica. The two steel-and-glass arenas contain an intriguing blend of the futuristic and something much older, hinting of the prehistoric, a kind of botanical Jurassic renaissance summoning the earliest of human notions of life on Earth. Here is a precious past brought to life in a captivating present, even as it heralds a new future.

With its two grounded, gigantic grid-shells, Gardens by the Bay resonates with the theme of ancient rebirth and future orientation, especially when compared with the adjacent landmark of the Marina Bay Sands SkyPark. Standing 57 storeys and 200 metres high in the sky across a road to the north, the integrated resort's boat-shaped roof terrace channels a futuristic airborne life support system straight out of a science-fiction movie. The metallic exoskeletons of the Gardens' two biomes, with their mammoth lattices of steel arches, look like exposed ribs. This aspect of symmetry is mirrored even further in the way that the domes' double shells create a structural dialogue with another pair of glass structures across the waters of Marina Bay — the twin domes that look like durians at the theatre and concert hall of Singapore's national arts centre, The Esplanade – Theatres on the Bay.

Inside the biomes, vast journeys of botanical discovery await. The twin key attractions on offer — access to the experience of perpetual spring, and exploring the abundant diversity of Mediterranean and montane plant life.

Gardens by the Bay resonates with the theme of ancient rebirth and future orientation, especially when compared with the adjacent landmark of the Marina Bay Sands SkyPark.

FLOWE

Perpetual spring in the Flower Dome

The larger biome, called the Flower Dome, is a cool-dry conservatory measuring 183 × 130 × 38 metres. The dome is 38 metres at its highest point, and at 1.2 hectares, it is about the size of two and a half football fields. Made up of 3,332 pieces of glass of 42 varying shapes and sizes, each is treated with low-emittance or 'low-e' coated glazing. In its design, the shape of the glass dome was tilted forward to create a wide, flat landscape typical of Mediterranean terrain. By contrast, its twin, the cool-moist dome, was shaped to exaggerate its height relative to its footprint towards one end where an artificial 'mountain' stands.

> THE FLOWER DOME REPRODUCES THE ENVIRONMENT OF A MEDITERRANEAN SPRING, KEEPING TO A CONSTANT TEMPERATURE RANGE OF 23 TO 25 DEGREES CELSIUS IN THE DAY AND 17 DEGREES IN THE NIGHT, AND WITH AROUND 70 PER CENT RELATIVE HUMIDITY.

The environment inside is suitable for plants that are common in the Mediterranean climate and also in semi-arid, sub-tropical regions. This climate is characterised by wet winters and dry summers lasting about half the year, with intense sunlight. A technical study of the prevailing light conditions in Singapore has shown that there is generally enough light to grow most of the Mediterranean plants here — even with only 65 per cent of sunlight being capable of penetrating the coated glazing of the glass dome roofs.

THE FLORA IN THE COOL-DRY CONSERVATORY HAILS FROM PLACES SUCH AS THE MEDITERRANEAN BASIN, WESTERN CAPE IN SOUTH AFRICA, MADAGASCAR, WESTERN AUSTRALIA, THE COASTAL PLAINS OF SOUTH AMERICA, AND CALIFORNIA IN THE WEST COAST OF NORTH AMERICA.

The flora in the cool-dry conservatory hails from places such as the Mediterranean basin, Western Cape in South Africa, Madagascar, Western Australia, the coastal plains of South America, and California in the west coast of North America. The plant displays tell different stories of how plants have adapted to the unique habitats of temperate climate zones.

The edutainment aspect is carried in the annotations to the displays, acting as footnotes to the entire immersion experience, giving context and meaning to this sensation of 'botanical teleportation' into these different plant worlds. Throughout the dome, global environmental concerns are addressed as part of the Gardens' overall thematic narratives, especially deforestation, habitat loss and climate change.

Taking centre stage below the arrival area into the dome is the Flower Field, which showcases seasonal displays of flowers and shrubs from different regions that flourish at different times of the year. These include plants from Europe, such as tulips and roses, as well as seasonal favourites such as chrysanthemums for Chinese New Year and poinsettias for Christmas.

The Baobabs display shows how baobabs, also known as bottle trees, overcome prolonged paucity of water with water-retention strategies such as swollen trunks to store water. The trees here come from continental Africa and Madagascar. Also here is the Succulent Garden, featuring water-retaining plants that have adapted to arid conditions, hence their fleshy or succulent appearance.

While the Californian Garden features plants such as the tree poppy and flannelbush that have showy flowers, other themed displays showcase Australian plants, including cat's paw, so-called because of their flower shapes. Some of the plants, such as the grass tree with leaves that look like grass, are very much part of Aboriginal history or have inspired indigenous artworks.

Featured plants in the South American Garden include the monkey puzzle tree, a conifer that is the national tree of Chile. In the Mediterranean Garden are similarly aged trees such as the olive trees. Another national plant is the giant protea, whose spectacular flower heads can be seen at the South African Garden.

The Olive Grove display looks at the cultivation, harvest and use of olives, how the fruit and oil of this versatile and valuable plant are piquant ingredients in many cuisines. Some of the trees here are over a thousand years old and originate from Spain.

Monkey puzzle tree in the South American Garden

Seascape in the Succulent Garden

Grass tree in the Australian Garden

Canary Island date palm

UNUSUAL PLANTS
of the Flower Dome

Adansonia digitata, or African baobab
Of the Malvaceae (cotton family) and native to the semi-arid sub-Saharan Africa, from Angola through Southern Africa and East Africa, reaching Sudan and Ethiopia, African baobab are massive deciduous trees that can reach up to 25 metres tall and 10 metres in diameter. The trunk is cylindrical or fluted, with buttresses topped by a spreading, rounded crown of branches. There are many uses for its roots, hollow trunks, bark, wood, leaves, flowers and fruit, from building materials to food and medicine. Its very nutritious leaves continue to be a staple diet for the African people.

Brachychiton rupestris, or Queensland bottle tree
Also of the Malvaceae and native to Australia, this 18 to 20-metre tall tree is especially useful to the Aborigines as a source of sustenance and raw materials. The starchy tissue of the stems, roots and seeds are edible. The roots also yield good quantities of drinking water. As with some baobabs, its fibrous bark is used to make rope and twine for fishing nets.

African baobab

Queensland bottle tree

Drunken tree

Italian cypress

Chilean wine palm

Madagascan ghost tree

Ceiba chodatii, the Argentinian Palo borracho or drunken tree
Again of the Malvaceae but native to Argentina, Bolivia and Paraguay, this small, bottle-shaped tree grows up to 12 metres tall. Related to the Kapok tree (*Ceiba pentandra*) of the Brazilian Amazon and Western Africa, the Palo borracho tree also has seeds surrounded by smooth, light fibres that are collected to make pillows and cushions.

Cupressus sempervirens, or Italian cypress
Of the Cupressaceae (cypress family) and native around the Mediterranean Sea, the Italian cypress reaches Switzerland in the north, south to Libya and east to Iran. The long-lasting, aromatic wood of this species has been used for millennia by many ancient civilisations, such as the Phoenicians and Cretans. The Egyptians built their sarcophagi with it, while the Greeks sculpted statues of their gods. It continues to be highly prized in more modern times, and is used, for example, for the doors of St Peter's Basilica in the Vatican City. Another product derived from this tree is cypress essential oil, distilled from its young stems and leaves, and used extensively in aromatherapy.

Jubaea chilensis, or Chilean wine palm
Of the Arecaceae (palm family) and native to Chile, this huge palm grows up to 30 metres tall, with a trunk reaching 1 metre in diameter. Also known as Coquito palm in Chile, its sap can be fermented into a palm wine or concentrated into a sweet syrup (palm honey) for culinary uses, rather similar to the *gula melaka* in Singapore. Although described somewhat disdainfully by Charles Darwin as a "very ugly tree", many consider the Chilean wine palm to be one of the most impressive palms in the world. One of the largest cultivated specimen is in a greenhouse at Kew Gardens, England.

Moringa drouhardii, or Madagascan ghost tree
Of the Moringaceae (horseradish tree family) and originally from southwestern Madagascar, this curious bottle-shaped tree grows up to 15 metres tall. Despite being related to the edible horseradish tree (*Moringa oleifera*) from India, its foliage, fruits and seeds appear not to be consumed locally. Its aromatic sap is sought-after for making medicines against colds and coughs.

[THE BAOBABS DISPLAY SHOWS HOW BAOBABS, ALSO KNOWN AS BOTTLE TREES, OVERCOME PROLONGED PAUCITY OF WATER WITH WATER-RETENTION STRATEGIES SUCH AS SWOLLEN TRUNKS TO STORE WATER.

[THE TREES FOR THE CONSERVATORIES HAVE TRAVELLED FAR, SOME TAKING AS LONG AS 60 DAYS FROM SOUTH AMERICA TO REACH SINGAPORE.

Montane plant life in the Cloud Forest

The other biome — the smaller but taller Cloud Forest — is the 123 × 95 × 58 metre and 0.8 hectare cool-moist conservatory that simulates the climate of tropical highlands.

These habitats are found in tropical mountain ranges between 1,000 and 3,500 metres above sea level, up to latitudes of 26 degrees north and south of the Equator. The constant daytime temperature range here is similar to that of the cool-dry biome at 23 to 25 degrees Celsius, but the relative humidity will be higher at around 80 per cent instead of 70 per cent. Sometimes described as 'every day a summer, every night a winter', the tropical montane climate is recreated in this dome environment that becomes progressively cooler and wetter with increasing elevation, except that with cool air being denser than hot air, the level at the ravine is the coolest in the conservatory.

The tropical montane displays feature flora from places such as Borneo (Mount Kinabalu), Costa Rica (Monteverde) and the mountain ranges of peninsular Malaysia (Cameron Highlands, Fraser's Hill and Maxwell Hill), showcasing the variety and versatility of plants from such microclimates.

The centrepiece of this conservatory is Crystal Mountain, an artificial mountain with a lookout at the peak. Accessible by elevator, this piece of high ground enables visitors to appreciate the flora of the montane regions while sauntering about in tropical city clothes, thus shedding the nuisance of having to wrestle with trekking gear or the irritation of insects.

Here are displayed magnolias, camellias and orchids as well as ericaceous plants such as rhododendrons which prefer soil that is more acidic and does not contain lime. Carnivorous plants such as pitcher plants and sundews feature against a carpet of delicate ferns and mosses. Descending level by level reveals different exhibitions within, and changing views out through the lattice to the landscape within the conservatory and beyond.

The Lower Forest Floor section, at the conservatory's ground level, depicts the region near to the limits of human habitation and the edge of wilderness, evoking the mystery, thrill and vast potential of a mist-enveloped frontier.

One section of the Lower Forest Floor showcases the Tea Tip Garden, featuring tea as a highland crop — its history, use, cultivation and production, as well as the threats to its environment. Other crops are featured here, including coffee and quinine, a plant indigenous to the Andes Mountains along western South America and which is cultivated in the tropics for medicinal properties including treating malaria and other afflictions.

Information displays explain how mountains are formed (their geology and tectonic plate movement) and their vital role in the Earth's functioning (in meteorology, weather systems and microclimates), as well as about stalagmites and stalactites in the cave exhibit, and the unusual plant and animal life in mountainous regions.

From here, an elevator ride up the mountain takes visitors into the 'Lost World' of the cloud forest at the very top. The other names of the cloud forest are no less evocative — mist-forest, montane rainforest and elfin forest, the last being the nickname for dwarfed forest ecosystems. The connotations of magic and mystique are entirely apt, for here is where the visitor will be enveloped by mist to simulate a cloud forest setting, another instance of technology enabling, and completing, the botanical verisimilitude. In this elevated seclusion, it is as if the plants here have taken full advantage of the licence afforded them by such splendid isolation at altitude, equipping them to give maximum expression to exuberant colour, variety and strangeness — as can be seen in plants such as the rhododendrons. The cloud forest functions like a sponge, storing water in the moss and soil that is released gradually. The specific effects of global warming on the cloud forest are highlighted. For instance, with higher sea surface temperatures, clouds would form at higher altitudes, thereby reducing overall moisture on the mountain, and plants in the lower sections of the cloud forest would die in the drier conditions.

This mountain peak, at 42 metres tall, is the second highest point of Gardens by the Bay. Two

> IN THE COOL-MOIST CONSERVATORY WHERE THE CRYSTAL MOUNTAIN STANDS, THE BIGGEST CHALLENGE WAS TO KEEP THE HIGHER LEVELS OF THE MOUNTAIN COOL ENOUGH.

elevated walkways traverse the mountainside — the Tree Top Walk (elevated on columns 13 metres off the ground and some 132 metres long) and the Cloud Walk (suspended from the gridshell at between 25 and 31 metres off the ground and some 122 metres long). The other circulation routes down from the top of the mountain are within the mountain lattice.

The peak is where visitors feel on top of the world, especially at the Cloud Walk and Tree Top Walk that allow them to explore the fantastic green-walling of the mountain and the canopies of trees and enjoy the sensation of spectacular elevation amongst the foliage. Here, mountain vistas will open up, far out, through the glass roof of the conservatory across to the city skyline, as well as deep inside, down to the view of the Secret Garden and a 40 metre-tall man-made waterfall, the world's highest such indoor attraction. As an additional feature to make the waterfall more realistic, there are 10 cataracts at different heights of the waterfall, from which water is discharged along the sides of the mountain face. Half of these openings are positioned at the top of the waterfall, with the rest at the mid and lower levels along the rock face. They can be adjusted to vary the form and force of the falling water.

Informative displays throughout the cool-moist conservatory focus on the main theme of the wilderness of the tropical mountain and the threats to its unique ecosystem, caused in some parts by expanding human agriculture and livestock grazing. The displays also address climate change issues and provide answers to questions such as "What if the Earth heats up by five degrees over the next century?" Interactive, large-scale imagery allows visitors to visualise the future and see how each degree change in temperature would affect the planet, with devastating scenarios ranging from the warmer sea water catalysing the mass bleaching of sea corals to the emergence of new deserts.

Moving from this scenario to behind the scenes, an interactive model of the Gardens by the Bay complex inside the mountain presents an overview of the natural cycles of the Gardens itself. Here, visitors will see the Gardens as a microcosm of planet Earth, and learn how the Gardens respects and implements measures to address the challenges of climate change, including sustainability, the water cycle, solar power, air and biomass, and the carbon imprint. Visitors can see the effect of rain, sun, air and earth on the Gardens.

The next section, the Secret Garden, showcases living fossils that have survived in sheltered environments — a story of an ancient, long-lost world told through relict species of prehistoric Gondwanaland, the super-continent that existed between 200 to 500 million years ago and included most of today's landmass in the southern hemisphere before they were separated by tectonic plate movements of the Earth's crust. The featured plants include the Wollemi pine, which was first found as a fossil and only recently as living specimens. This plant's closest relatives may be South American species of *Araucaria* such as the monkey puzzle tree from Chile. This common ancestry dates to an ancient time when Australia, Antarctica and South America were linked by land.

Ferns are another example of relicts, which first appeared as fossils in the early-Carboniferous period, 360 to 300 million years ago, known as 'the Land of the Giants'; it was a time when oxygen levels were at their highest ever on Earth and towering trees and huge insects such as spiders with 18-inch legs were found everywhere. A clue to the prehistoric heritage of these plants is that they do not produce flowers or seeds, but are reproduced by spores. These spores germinate in shady, moist areas, forming a delicate plant that bears gametes. The male gamete, or sperm, swims to fertilise the female gamete, or ovule, giving origin to a fern plant on that spot.

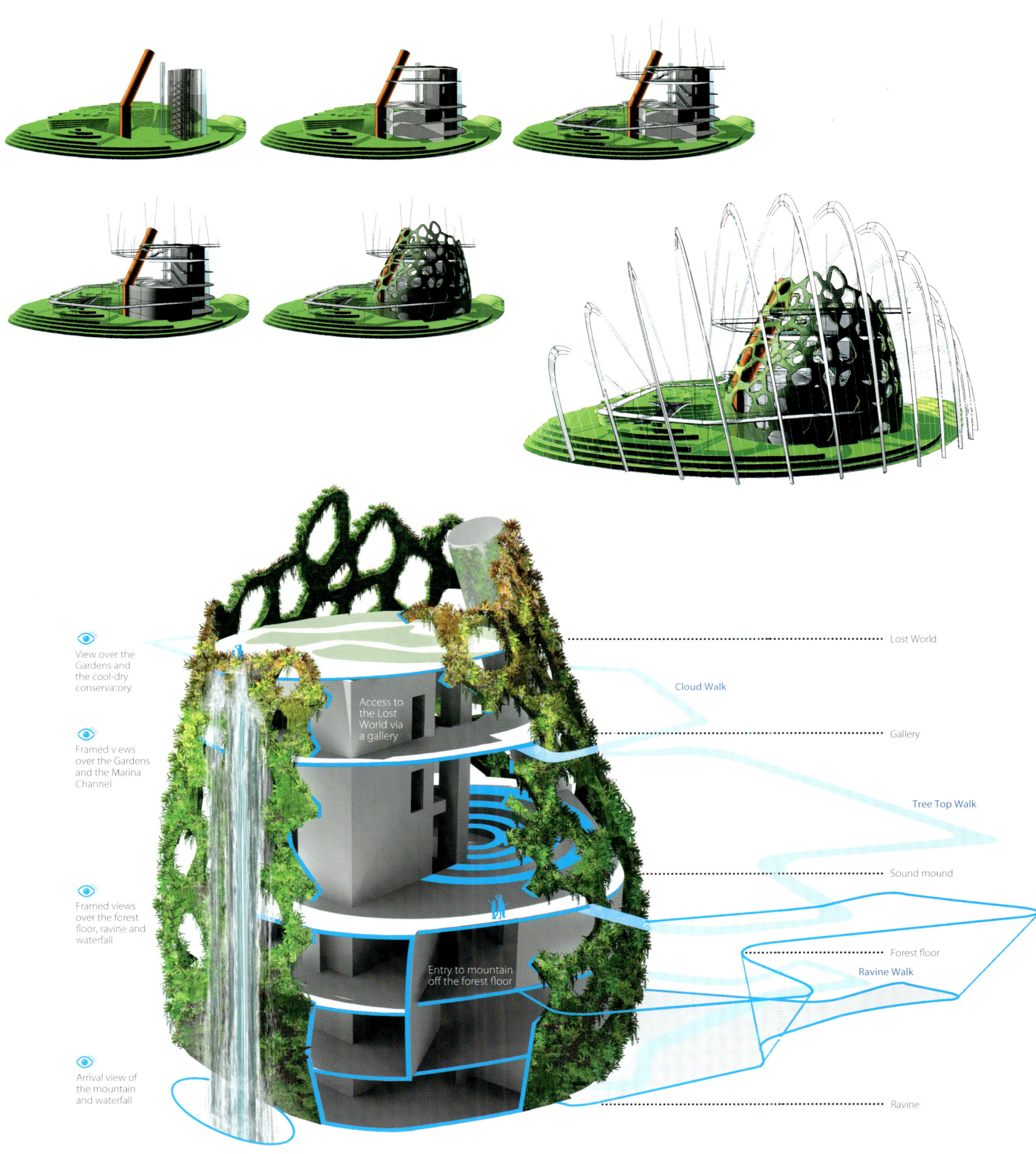

A section of the 42-metre-tall Crystal Mountain planted with bromeliads and anthuriums

Tiger orchid

Pitcher plant

Maidenhair fern

Tree fern

[THE DISPLAYS IN THE CLOUD FOREST ADDRESS CLIMATE CHANGE ISSUES AND PROVIDE ANSWERS TO QUESTIONS SUCH AS "WHAT IF THE EARTH HEATS UP BY FIVE DEGREES OVER THE NEXT CENTURY?"

The peak is where visitors feel on the Cloud Walk and Tree Top Walk.

top of the world especially at

A floral United Nations

The plants of the conservatories are a veritable botanical United Nations. While they come from nurseries from all over the world, the species themselves hail from countries as diverse as Madagascar, Argentina, United States, China, Peru, Ecuador, Costa Rica and many others.

The longest journeys from South America would have taken some 60 days to reach Singapore. Indeed, the size of the plants was only restrained — in the end — by a rather mundane constraint. In transporting the plants by trailer within Singapore, the largest tree that could be moved could not have a root bore (with the plant lying on its side) of more than 3.5 metres in diameter. Including the height of the flat bed or trailer would add up to just under 4.5 metres in height — the limit passable under Singapore's overhead bridges and electronic road pricing gantries.

If size is limited, however, variety is guaranteed. In the Flower Field within the Flower Dome, which is dedicated to changing displays, the plants will be changed three to four times a year, and the accent in the displays will be on colourful abundance, with, for example, 10,000 buds of chrysanthemums opening all at once. Before the plants took their place in the Gardens, some of them waited in the wings at the prototype glasshouses during the Gardens' construction. Planting started in the cool-dry conservatory in April 2011 and in the cool-moist one in March 2012.

An unexpected additional success factor for the Gardens were the plant suppliers themselves, some of whom early on shared in the passion and vision of Gardens by the Bay. Many were willing, and in some cases, eager, to hold the plants in their own inventory for as long as was required, especially those that had been procured long before their eventual delivery into the conservatories or other new homes within the Gardens.

The kaleidoscope of colour that is the Gardens by the Bay was put together by practically scouring the Earth. The plant sourcing trips covered places including the USA, South Africa, Madagascar, Argentina, Uruguay, Spain, Italy, Canary Islands and China. The trips brought their share of unusual experiences. Andrew Grant, who masterplanned the Bay South Garden and went on some of the plant sourcing trips with the Gardens' botanists and horticulturists, recalls waking early one morning and being startled to see a fossa, a catlike creature in the mongoose family that is endemic to Madagascar. He only later realised that it was kept as a pet by the locals who were travelling with the team. On another occasion, while sourcing for stones in a small village in China, he was offered scorpions for a meal. He declined the local delicacy, but took away a lasting memory.

Ng Boon Gee, Assistant Director (Gardens Operations) at the Gardens, recalls a harrowing experience in Thailand. The team had been travelling for a few hours to a nursery in the countryside when the driver suddenly announced the van was running out of petrol. Luckily for them, a villager was helpful and got them some petrol. It was almost 8 pm by the time they reached the nursery, and they had to select the plants in darkness. The drive back was just as harrowing — on pitch-dark roads and, at one point, against the flow of traffic.

Fooling the flowers

Sometimes, beauty is the fruit of deception. At the cooled conservatories of Gardens by the Bay, by lowering temperatures for a month from 17 to 13 degrees Celsius at night, horticulturists hope to hoodwink the plants inside into believing that they have gone through winter, before raising the temperature to trigger them to flower in readiness for spring. Not only that, this 'trick' will be performed a few times a year to create what would be a wonderland of perpetual spring all year round.

This stunning show of constant colour was made possible only with elaborate preparation and 'rehearsals' stretching a few years beforehand. The location for all this backstage work was half a dozen prototype glasshouses at Pasir Panjang in the western part of Singapore, at another National Parks Board facility called HortPark. The glasshouses were built in 2006 as an experimental 'living laboratory' to fine-tune the best ways to replicate optimum conditions for plants in the cool-dry and cool-moist climates of the conservatories.

The prototype glasshouses are test-beds for simulating seasonal fluctuations including factors that can easily be neglected, such as the average length of day in different seasons. In Singapore, the shortest day of the year is about 11 hours and 50 minutes, and the longest, 12 hours and 10 minutes — a difference of less than half an hour. By contrast, in places further from the Equator such as Sydney, Cape Town and Miami, the difference between the shortest and longest days can be three to four hours. Because plants take their cue on when to bloom from day-lengths, this aspect also has to be simulated to complete the deception, but this is harder to achieve at the actual site, given the transparency of the glass domes. The other alternative is to look for plants that respond more to other factors such as temperature and availability of water.

Four of the glasshouses have temperatures and humidity similar to springtime in the Mediterranean and semi-arid sub-tropical regions of Spain, France, Greece, Western Australia and California. Plants from these regions include lavender, rosemary, olives, figs, grapes, geraniums and snapdragons. The other two glasshouses simulate cloud forests in the tropics at altitudes between 1,000 and 3,500 metres, such as at Mount Kinabalu in Borneo, and Genting Highlands and Cameron Highlands in peninsular Malaysia. Plants from these regions include Vireya rhododendrons, fuchsias, begonias and African violets.

Prototype glasshouses at HortPark off Alexandra Road were used to test-bed climate control and other sustainability features for the two cooled conservatories at Gardens by the Bay

A microcosm of multiculturalism

Vibrant cosmopolitanism has always been an abiding hallmark of the island of Singapore. So too is it a feature of the cooled conservatories of Gardens by the Bay. Ever since Sir Thomas Stamford Raffles and the British colonialists of the 19th century declared the former fishing village an "emporium of the East", it has been a thriving magnet for migrants, with people from China, India and elsewhere arriving to seek their fortunes, aiming to prosper in a conducive new habitat — just like the imported plants of Gardens by the Bay now aspire to do.

> THE NATIONAL FLOWER, AN ORCHID, ALSO EPITOMISES THE PRE-EMINENCE OF COSMOPOLITANISM IN THIS GARDENS COMPLEX AS MUCH AS IN THE COUNTRY.

Some of the orchids grown in the Cloud Forest, (from left) *Coelogyne fimbriatum*, *Cattleya iricolor*, *Cattleya maxima* and *Anguloa clowesii*

In the 21st century, Singapore has taken its multiculturalism up a few levels, attracting immigrants and investors alike from much farther afield — from as far away as the Middle East and Eastern Europe — as international transport has become easier. By way of extended metaphor, Gardens by the Bay can be seen as a botanical version of the microcosm of multiculturalism that is Singapore. The two cooled conservatories are the primary physical emblems of this symbolism.

The national flower, an orchid, also epitomises the pre-eminence of cosmopolitanism in this Gardens complex as much as in the country. As Andrew Grant, designer of the Bay South Garden, says, the orchid was his original inspiration for the masterplan design which he submitted for the international design competition in 2006. "Orchids are found all over the world," he observes, citing yet another aspect of globalisation about this fragile yet resilient flower.

Another point that one could add is that, just as the resourceful orchid can manage to survive in arid, rocky places, drawing nutrients from the air through its own roots, so too, the Gardens, built on reclaimed land, have enabled an abundance of flora to thrive on a man-made surface, relying on human ingenuity to overcome the many design challenges. This feature of diligent and resourceful triumph over adversity is also a country brand attribute of Singapore, which has always strived to overcome its limitations with imagination and application.

To Grant, the orchid also represents the essence of Gardens by the Bay itself, and this sense of the plant's significance is invested spatially into something as concrete (literally) as the very layout of the place. Facets of the orchid fan out across the geometry of the whole site, with the paths that interlace the Gardens stretching out like the exposed roots of this epiphyte, its stems reaching out in zig-zag patterns in-between the 'buds' of the Gardens' various site attractions. The whole Gardens is a kind of "art project informed by science", Grant says, fully aware that the conservatories, for instance, would never work unless the science was right.

Vanda 'John Clubb' in the Colonial Garden, chosen for its floriferousness and free-flowering characteristics

A coup for green architecture

While the botanical stars deservedly hog the spotlight at these wondrous biomes, there is another dimension to marvel at — the human ingenuity that made the conservatories possible. The twin structures were designed by Wilkinson Eyre Architects, together with designers Grant Associates and two other British engineering firms, Atelier One and Atelier Ten. Atelier had worked on the designs of projects in Singapore including Clarke Quay and The Esplanade – Theatres on the Bay. In total, 21 specialist consultants were engaged on a range of aspects, including environmental sustainability, climate engineering, geo-technical, soil design, irrigation, facade, wind, acoustics and vibrations, fire engineering, interpretive media, way-finding, crowd dynamics and insurance. They hailed from all over the world, including Britain, Germany, Japan and Australia.

In the process of addressing the engineering design requirements of the conservatories, the team encountered many challenges. First, they had to accommodate the weight of the buildings themselves, calculated to be around 720 tonnes each, by factoring this into the ground foundations.

The next most significant factor was the wind, especially local draught pockets that can exert a focused force on a particular section of the domes. The arches or ribs of the grid-shells give support in a way not too different from the cross-ridges found on seashells, which give the molluscs their durability. As approvals were being sought from the building authorities, it was found that some requirements, inherited from decades-old British codes of practice in the building industry, were based on archaic considerations such as designing for snow load. These regulations were eventually reduced, though not entirely removed.

In what is a coup for green architecture, the carbon emissions of the cooled conservatories are kept close to that of a complex of commercial buildings of the same footprint size. The primary task was to calibrate the temperature and humidity differentials between ambient and internal conditions in the most effective and cost-efficient manner — so as to recreate the most hospitable new homes possible for the transported plants. The aim was to create 'living buildings' that are responsive to the changeable Singaporean weather — always hot, sometimes sunny, but often cloudy. This was the main aspect for which the project's foreign consultants had to take time to adapt to local conditions and to find design and engineering solutions. As Paul Baker, director at Wilkinson Eyre and chief architect for the project, observes: "The forms are designed to minimise the envelope — like bubbles, they have minimal surface area for the volume enclosed."

There was yet another important challenge — to manage the conditions so that humans can be comfortable too. Since the entire temperature range in the plants' natural habitats could go as low as 7 degrees Celsius, it was decided that the Gardens would focus on replicating only the optimal temperatures, thus creating substantial savings in cooling efforts. However, tweaking the temperature periodically is necessary to induce blooming — a shift in temperatures down to between 10 and 17 degrees Celsius periodically at night is needed to trigger the physiological conditions for flowering.

The first step was to manage the inflow of solar energy and to balance this against the light levels that are needed for horticulture. The systems make best use of the laws of physics, in particular, the tendency for warm air to rise. Cool air is introduced at low levels around the perimeter and within the plant beds. At the same time, a network of pipes embedded in the pathways absorbs heat from the sun, preventing stone surfaces from heating up and re-radiating into the space — part of the phenomenon known as the greenhouse effect. The two systems combined keep the conservatories cool and comfortable for both people and plants.

[THE ARCHES OR RIBS OF THE GRID-SHELLS GIVE SUPPORT IN A WAY NOT TOO DIFFERENT FROM THE CROSS-RIDGES FOUND ON SEASHELLS, WHICH GIVE THE MOLLUSCS THEIR DURABILITY.

Cooling the conservatories

To advance sustainability and minimise carbon emissions from the glass domes, environmental engineers had to work out the best way to dehumidify and cool the large amounts of fresh air needed to keep the indoor temperature comfortable for both people and plants. To take the cooling of the conservatories off the electrical grid, the solution was to use renewable fuel and liquid desiccant. External air is introduced to subterranean plant rooms through a cowl at the rear of the conservatories, slightly above ground level. Here, desiccants remove most of the moisture from the air (from 90 to 30 per cent relative humidity) before it is cooled by piped chilled water.

The main energy source used for dehumidifying and cooling the air in the domes comes from a 15-metre-tall biomass plant located in the Gardens' energy centre near the main entrance. Within this biomass plant, wood chips are burnt to produce superheated steam which is used to generate electricity. The waste heat from the power generation process is then used to regenerate the desiccants by 'boiling' off the moisture that has been accumulated. Flue gases from the boiler are carefully cleaned before being released to the atmosphere through chimneys inside the cluster of three Supertrees located near the Gardens' main entrance. The desiccant regeneration exhaust pipes are concealed in another cluster of Supertrees near the Dragonfly Lake. The waste heat also serves the absorption chillers which, along with electric chillers powered from the CHP (combined heat and power) unit, generate the chilled water needed to cool the buildings.

The primary fuel source for the biomass system comes from some 5,000 tonnes of waste wood. This waste wood is collected every month by the National Parks Board from the three million trees that it looks after in the parks and on the streets of the island. The cycle of life is further completed with waste being turned into nutrient, as ash from the boiler is mixed with the park's vegetation clippings and used as compost. Being able to make use of this natural waste material — one that could be converted into 'free energy' — turned what seemed a crazy idea of building cooled conservatories of this size on the Equator into a remarkable environmental story.

In the cool-moist conservatory where the Crystal Mountain stands, the biggest challenge was to keep the higher levels of the mountain cool enough. While the Forest Floor and lower levels of the mountain are cooled via a process called displacement cooling, where cooler air displaces warmer air, there was a need to ensure that enough cooler air could reach the higher levels. Because warm air rises naturally, a hybrid ventilation system had to be added. This included displacement air outlets at the mountain's peak and base, and jet diffusers concealed on the slopes to blast out cooled air to prevent the hot air from stratifying at the intermediate level. Evaporative misters add a fine spray of water to increase the humidity where needed. The aerial walkways also have misters on their undersides to add to the effect of evaporative cooling. The water droplets released from the misters absorb heat as they evaporate.

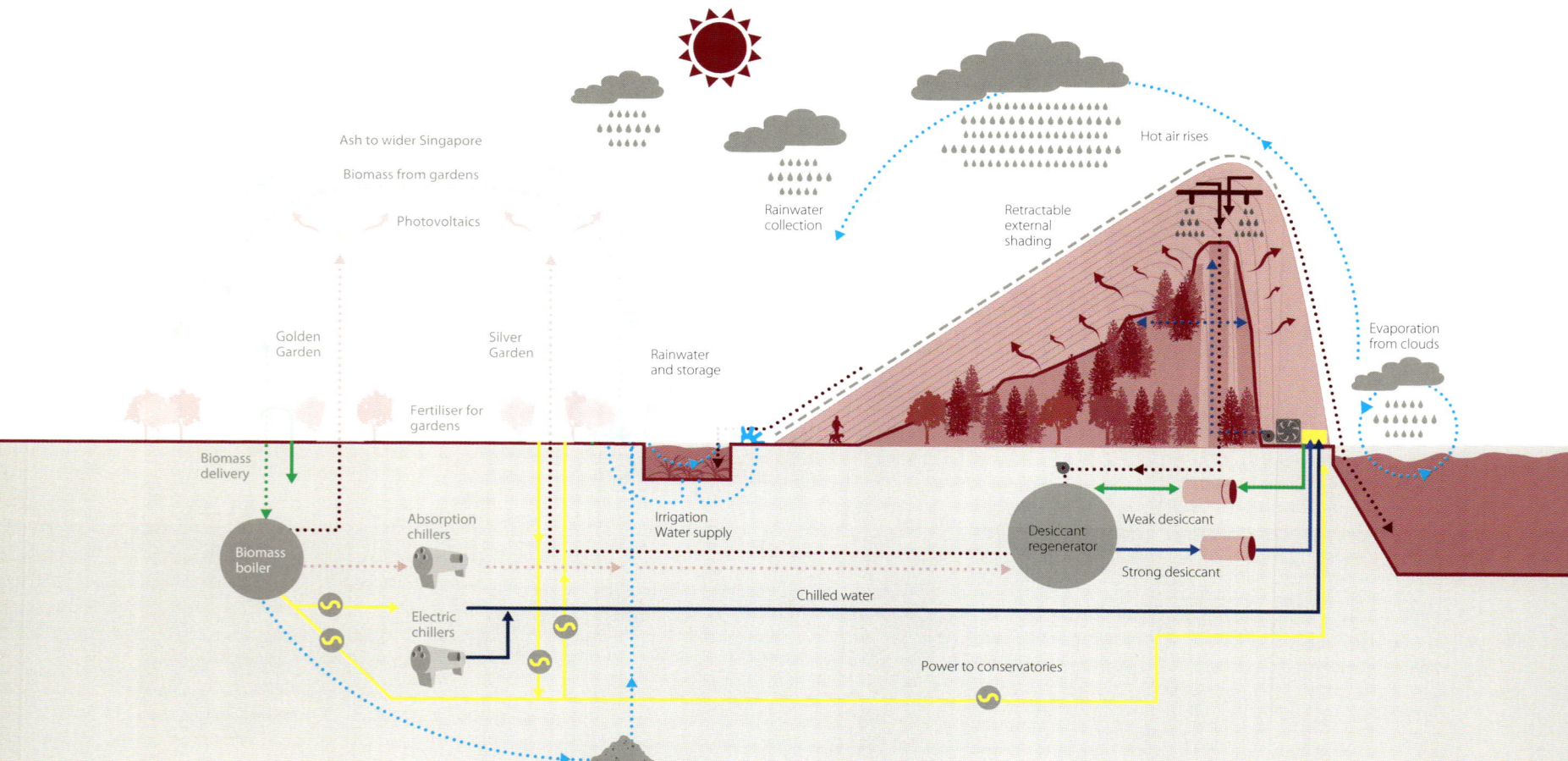

Form & Geometry

Sun path
Shading
Indirect sunlight
Reflected sunlight

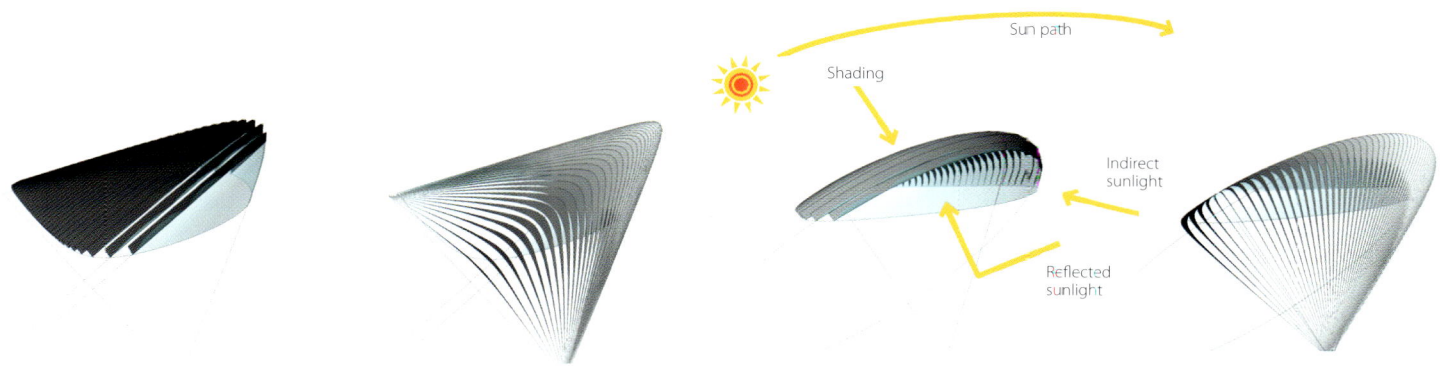

Shading & Structure

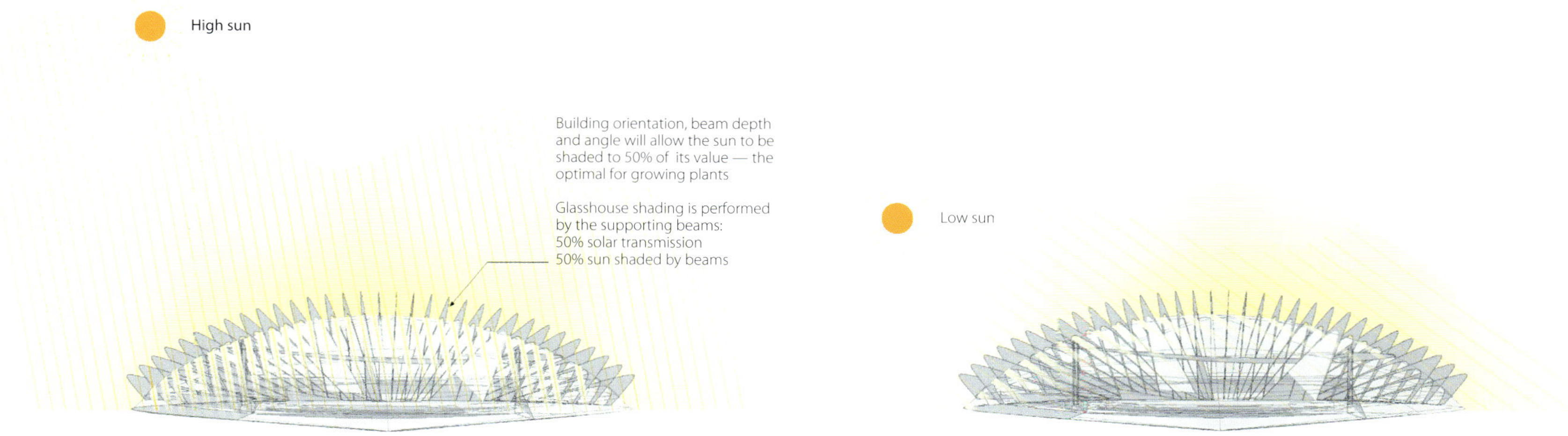

High sun
Building orientation, beam depth and angle will allow the sun to be shaded to 50% of its value — the optimal for growing plants
Glasshouse shading is performed by the supporting beams:
50% solar transmission
50% sun shaded by beams
Low sun

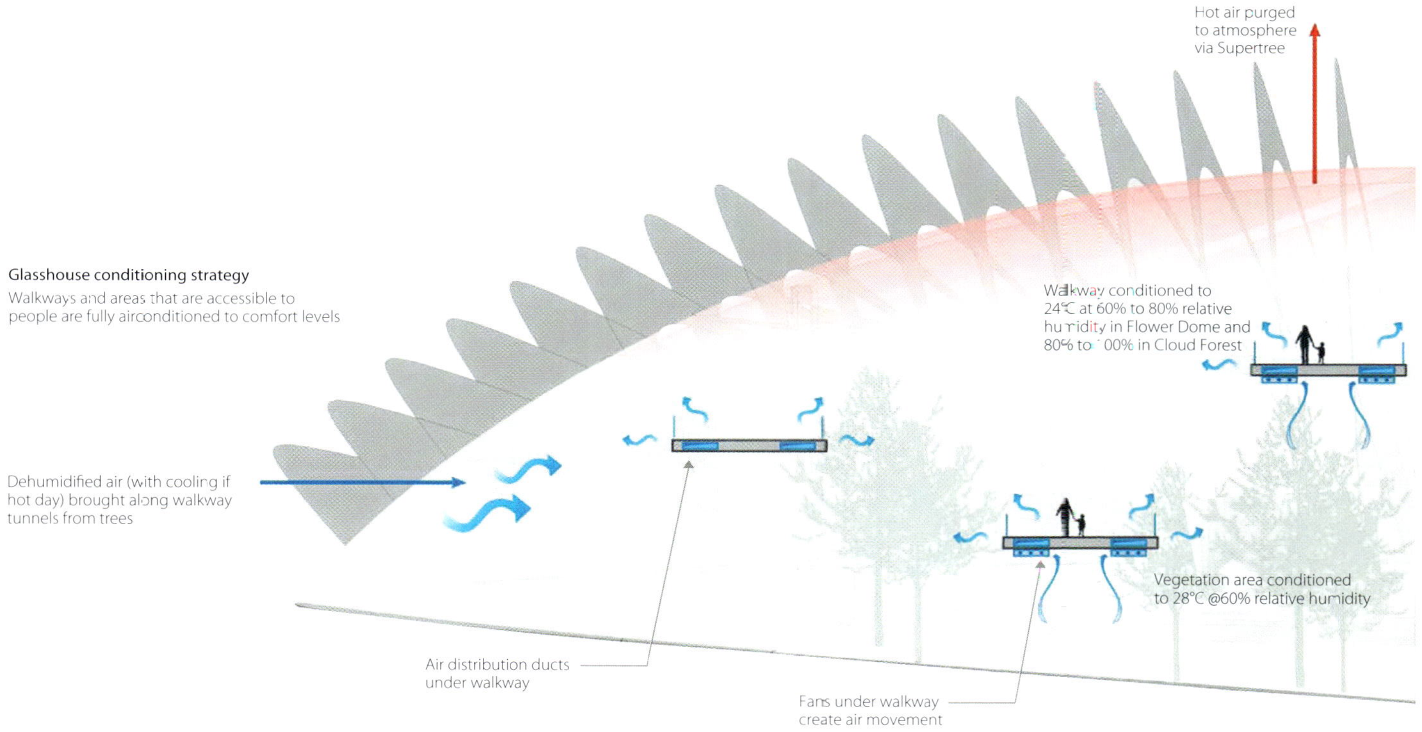

Hot air purged to atmosphere via Supertree
Glasshouse conditioning strategy
Walkways and areas that are accessible to people are fully airconditioned to comfort levels
Walkway conditioned to 24°C at 60% to 80% relative humidity in Flower Dome and 80% to 100% in Cloud Forest
Dehumidified air (with cooling if hot day) brought along walkway tunnels from trees
Vegetation area conditioned to 28°C @60% relative humidity
Air distribution ducts under walkway
Fans under walkway create air movement

Warmth and light for the plants

The comfort of the plants was the key consideration for the cooled conservatories. A National Parks Board study, led by CPGreen consultant Dr Nirmal Krishnani and Dr Wolfgang Kessling of German climate engineering firm Transolar Energietechnik GmbH, found that for the plants to flourish, the light levels in the conservatories should be kept in excess of 45,000 lux for more hours than the benchmark levels at the Eden Project in Cornwall and Kew Gardens in London, England.

Extra light is allowed to filter in because of the remarkable technique employed in the external design, which allows the conservatories not to have any internal columns despite their size, and so, to avoid the shadows that supporting pillars would have cast. The glass domes are suspended from the external ribs that provide support, and yet from a distance, the domes look 'detached' from the glass.

Another challenge was to minimise the shadows that would be cast by the supporting ribs. Lighting conditions therefore had to be engineered such that, for instance, the less sunny north-facing sides of the biomes would also draw from sunlight reflected off the waters of the Marina Channel. Singapore is incredibly humid, and the sky is either overcast or very bright. In short, usually there is either too little or too much sun. The double-glazed glass panes on the domes' facades let in 65 per cent of daylight but only 35 per cent of solar heat, which is what contributes to the cooling load. The low-emissivity coatings on the panes' inner face are virtually invisible.

Having to balance the need for as much light as possible on frequent cloudy days with the high equatorial sun on clear days led to the development of an automated retractable shading system for the arched grid-shells of the conservatories' domes. Developed by Wilkinson Eyre Architects and CPG Consultants, together with other firms including Meinhardt Infrastructure, Atelier One and Singapore contractor Woh Hup, the shades on the conservatory complex are different from those on The Esplanade – Theatres on the Bay in that the shades move. They are part of a dynamic, responsive system and will change position as the weather changes to control the amount of direct sunlight entering the domes. The shades are made of many pieces of coated polyester fibre fabric, and are of triangular shape partly to fit the shape of the dome and its ribs, and also to create a pleasing look. The 'fins' vary in size to fit each side of each panel all across the arching domes, with the largest pieces (the ones at the tops of the domes) measuring 7 × 10 metres. The shades were designed to completely disappear into the ribs, so as to not increase the amount of shade cast when not in use. This ensures that when as much light as possible is needed, the only shade comes from the absolutely necessary (but lightest possible) structure and nothing else.

When activated by light-sensitive sensors, these panels will be like a responsive skin with a series of sails unfurling from the steel ribs of the supporting structures. The visual effect, when all the shades are unfurled, will be of two gigantic pinecones. In its own way of cultural symmetry and appropriateness, the botanical metaphor of a pinecone — a fruit from temperate climates — will be an apt and attractive complement to the two other huge domes across the opposite bank of Marina Bay, which are compared with another fruit, the tropical 'durians' of The

Preliminary concept model of Flower Dome structure

Esplanade – Theatres on the Bay. One major difference, though, is that the conservatories' shading system will project flat 'sails' instead of the protruding spikes on the Esplanade's domes.

In designing Gardens by the Bay primarily for the plants, there were creative tensions that had to be resolved between the foreign consultants and those based in Singapore, including CPG Consultants, Meinhardt Infrastructure and the project managers PM Link.

In the long process of project management, one of the major points of difference was the tension, on some levels, between aesthetics and physics. In the case of the conservatories, this applied to the design of the arches on the exterior of the domes. Visually, the arches look as if they are 'pulling up' the glass domes and thus supporting their weight, when in fact the domes stand essentially on their own and the arches' main function is to protect the biomes from lateral movement caused by the wind. A balance had to be sought between the original design intent to keep the arches slim and sleek, and the perhaps more traditional school of thought that prioritises structural stability more and would have preferred to see more of the load to be distributed to the arches. But this would have made the 'ribs' and the struts look thicker and perhaps less attractive.

This creative tension — in essence, a divide between big and small — also applied to the trees that were planned for the Gardens. The consultants from Europe were used to having trees in paved areas planted inside holes in the ground that are about 1.5 metres in diameter. Among other reasons, tree holes of this size helped to keep gardens looking neater. But many of the trees that were brought in were bigger. In the end, the tree holes such as those at the promenade along the waterfront were enlarged to 2 and even 3 metres in diameter. Inside the conservatories, tree holes were abandoned in favour of planter beds to house the trees in the various sections of the domes.

TO ADVANCE SUSTAINABILITY AND MINIMISE CARBON EMISSIONS FROM THE GLASS DOMES, ENVIRONMENTAL ENGINEERS HAD TO WORK OUT THE BEST WAY TO DEHUMIDIFY AND COOL THE LARGE AMOUNTS OF FRESH AIR NEEDED TO KEEP THE INDOOR TEMPERATURE COMFORTABLE FOR BOTH PEOPLE AND PLANTS.

[WHILE THE BOTANICAL STARS DESERVEDLY HOG THE SPOTLIGHT, THERE IS ANOTHER DIMENSION TO MARVEL AT — THE HUMAN INGENUITY THAT MADE THE CONSERVATORIES POSSIBLE.

Inside the biomes, vast journeys

of botanical discovery await.

4
The Supertrees
Green Giants, Vertical Gardens

These giant trees and vertical gardens sum up the symbolic essence of the Gardens as a fusion of nature, art and technology.

> WITH BARK AND BRANCHES OF STEEL, THESE MAN-MADE TREES SUPPORT 'LIVING SKINS' OF LUSH VERTICAL PLANTING.

Next to the two cooled glass conservatories, 18 magnificent tree-like structures some 25 to 50 metres (or between nine and 16 storeys) tall — aptly named Supertrees — are the most prominent, inviting features of Gardens by the Bay.

Twelve of these Supertrees take pride of place in the Supertree Grove in the centre of the Bay South Garden. The remaining six are located near the conservatories alongside the Dragonfly Lake and at the Arrival Square. Not only are the towering Supertrees botanical marvels with a big difference in being fashioned by man, they also stand tall in addressing some of the key environmental concerns of the 21st century.

These giant trees and vertical gardens sum up — quintessentially — the symbolic essence of the Gardens as a fusion of nature, art and technology. They embody the key aspects of the design concept created by Grant Associates, the designers of the Gardens at Bay South, working with the project's other firms including CPG Consultants and Meinhardt Infrastructure of Singapore. Erected on a foundation and inner core of concrete, and stretching out to the sky with bark and branches of steel, these man-made trees support 'living skins' of lush vertical planting, creating an epiphytic wonderland that is also a mini laboratory of sustainability, a test-bed to replicate the many cycles of nature.

The Hanging Gardens redefined

Gardens by the Bay is emblematic of Singapore's City in a Garden vision as the island republic expands on the earlier Garden City model. Now, flora and greenery embrace the city more fully and organically — just as flesh covers bone. Likewise, the man-made woodland of the Supertrees stands as pillars of concrete within, but without, those concrete 'tree trunks' support planted panels up to 40 metres in height, each lushly draped with ferns, orchids and climbers.

Housing nearly 163,000 plants from 30 countries, the Supertrees stand like a modern-day reinterpretation of the ancient vision of a Hanging Gardens of Babylon, even as their steel branches announce their futuristic origin as they stretch out into the sky. The plants growing on the Supertrees include more than 200 species, varieties and cultivars, including bromeliads (such as *Tillandsia stricta* from Brazil and *Tillandsia fasciculata* from Panama), orchids (*Cattleya maxima* from Ecuador), tropical flowering climbers and *Pseudorhipsalis*, a cactus from Costa Rica.

> HOUSING NEARLY 163,000 PLANTS FROM 30 COUNTRIES, THE SUPERTREES STAND LIKE A MODERN-DAY REINTERPRETATION OF THE ANCIENT VISION OF A HANGING GARDENS OF BABYLON.

There is a wonderful symmetry in the Supertrees between Man and Nature in that, much as cutting-edge human construction seeks to reach for the clouds in building the ever-higher skyscraper, so too, botanical life is about each plant striving to extend itself against other plants in eternal photosynthetic one-upmanship for sunlight and moisture in the atmosphere.

The Supertrees, their trunks wrapped in luxuriant vegetation, bring this affinity home in an intriguing harmony of humanity and horticulture. These supports are man-made artifice, but the facilitation for ascent that they provide acts as intriguing enhancements on nature by fashioning innovative habitats for plants to perch on. At the same time, like tall trees in nature, the Supertrees will also provide shade from the sun for visitors strolling on the pathways below.

PLANTING STRATEGY IN THE SUPERTREE

Base structure and panels

Base planting : green epiphytes + climbers
Accent planting : bromeliads
Accent colour : yellow

Base planting : mixed bromeliads
Accent planting : green climbers
Feature planting : large bromeliads + orchids

Base planting : green epiphytes + climbers
Accent planting : bromeliads
Accent colour : red

GROVE

FULL MOCK-UP

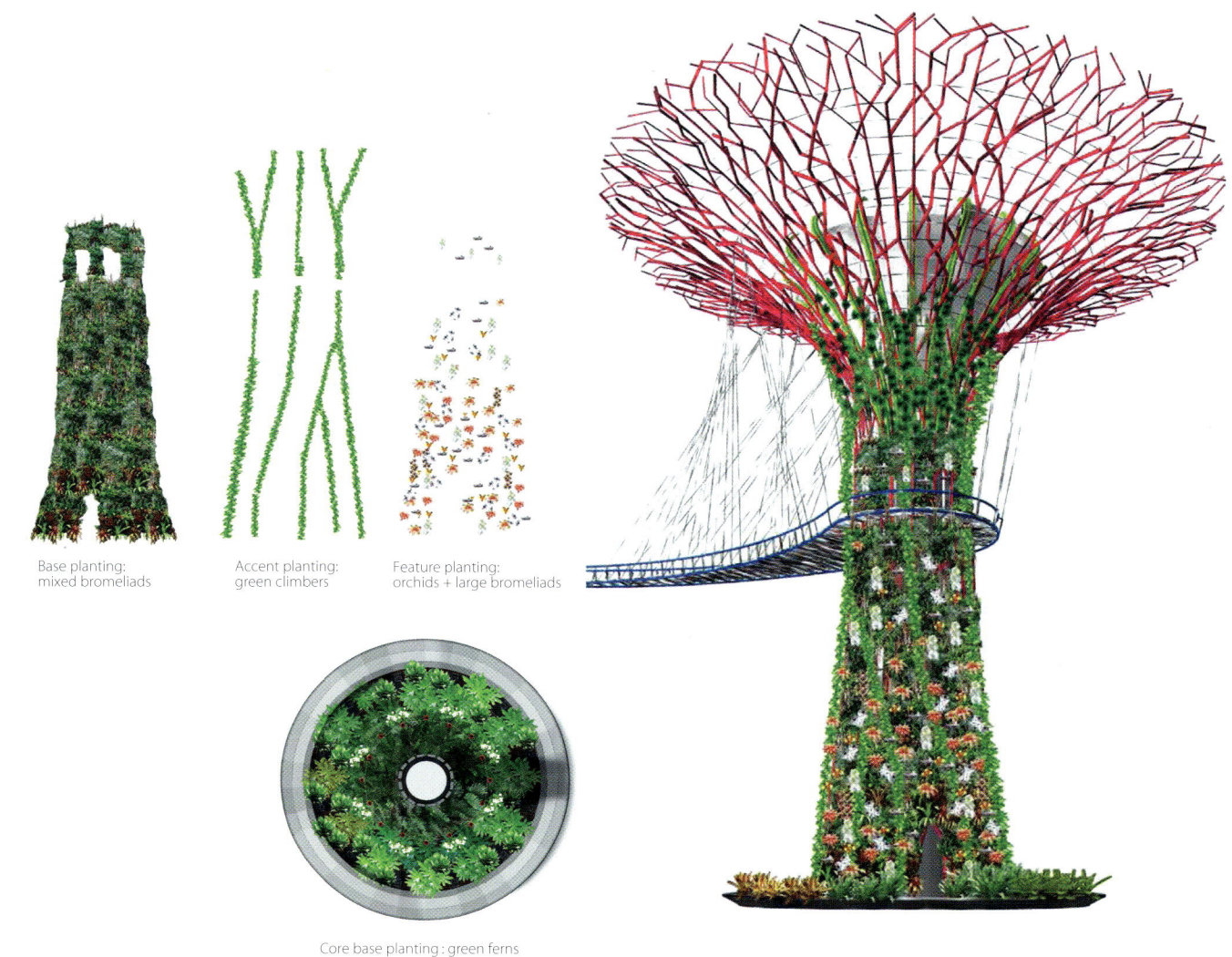

Base planting: mixed bromeliads

Accent planting: green climbers

Feature planting: orchids + large bromeliads

Core base planting : green ferns
Accent planting   : green epiphytes

Bromeliads: The star epiphytes

Of the 163,000 plants on the 18 Supertrees, most are chosen for their botanical interest, visual appeal and colour. Most are epiphytes, plants that rely on other plants for physical support, a role replicated by the concrete and steel of the Supertrees. Examples include the air plant *Tillandsia stricta* to give a silver colour for the cluster of three Supertrees by the Dragonfly Lake, and the bromeliad *Neoregelia* 'Grace' for hues of orange, brown, green, red and pink for those in the Supertree Grove.

If the Supertrees, together with the cooled conservatories, are the stars of Gardens by the Bay, the star plants of the Supertrees are the bromeliads, with their brightly coloured and patterned foliage, and long-lasting flowers opening in succession on the flower stem or accompanied by colourful bracts. By day, the Supertrees are like fantastical and gigantic jewellery stands for these bromeliad necklaces of green and multi-coloured gemstones. Nightfall and clever lighting further amplify their resplendence.

Bromeliads are primarily epiphytic in that they grow on tree limbs and take all their nourishment from the atmosphere, rain and falling leaf litter. They require a very lightweight soil mix, or none at all, making them prime candidates for vertical planting. Living high on tree limbs, where water evaporates quickly after rainfall, bromeliads have developed special ways to retain water. As the main feature plant on all 18 Supertrees, the bromeliads have a lot of vertical surface to cover — up to 70 per cent of the height of the concrete structures.

Helping the bromeliads to settle fully into Singapore will take time. Harry Luther, Assistant Director (Research) at Gardens by the Bay, believes that experimentation will be needed for many years to approximate the optimum conditions of nature at this horticultural showpiece. Continuous calibration will be needed to adjust to changing conditions, for instance, knowing exactly when to turn off the water supply to simulate the dry season.

Luther, who has over 30 years' experience working with epiphytes, marvels at the vast diversity of these plants, whose places of origin include Brazil and Peru. Some are not yet scientifically catalogued; some were only recently named, like the showy, pink-bracted *Vriesea kentii* christened in late 2010. Colour and variety of form will create a visual delight at the Supertree Grove. And, as if this rich array by day were not enough, the flowers will be "1,000 per cent different" at night, he promises, with special lighting effects making them even more attractive.

Apart from bromeliads and orchids, to add even more texture and biodiversity, the Supertrees are also adorned with other epiphytes such as aroids, cacti and hoyas, as well as climbers including bougainvilleas, quis-qualis and bauhinias.

Types of bromeliad

Bromeliads are members of the plant family Bromeliaceae named after the 15th-century Swedish physician Olaus Bromelius. With some 3,200 species named, bromeliads rank somewhere mid-table in rankings of about 400 families created by taxonomists to catalogue the 350,000 known kinds of all flowering plants.

There are two basic forms of epiphytic bromeliads — tank and air types. Tank types have rosettes of overlapping leaves (like the bird's nest fern) which overlap so efficiently that they can hold precious water. Atmospheric types do not hold water. Instead, they have trichomes, or little scales, on their foliage that often appear like dense silver fur. While also reflecting sunlight, these fine-textured scales also trap water by capillary action, much like the drying effect of a terry-cloth towel after a shower.

> EXPERIMENTATION WILL BE NEEDED FOR MANY YEARS TO APPROXIMATE THE OPTIMUM CONDITIONS OF NATURE FOR THESE BROMELIADS.

Tillandsia ionantha var. *maxima*

Aechmea chantinii

Tillandsia stricta

Neoregelia 'Tangerine'

Oncidium Gower Ramsey 'Golden Wish'

Bromeliaceae (pineapple family)

Tillandsia ionantha var. *maxima*. This very large growing variety (more than twice the size of the common type of the species) is found on the ancient lava flows in western Mexico.

Aechmea chantinii. This bromeliad is widespread in the Amazon, where it grows on trees in hot, humid forests. It was lost to cultivation for many years but was rediscovered in the early 1960s. Its red, orange and yellow inflorescence lasts for months.

Tillandsia stricta. This is a widespread tropical American air plant. The main type at the Supertrees comes from the coastal scrubby forests just north of Rio de Janeiro, Brazil, where it flowers off and on all year.

Neoregelia 'Tangerine'. This is a Florida, USA, hybrid of unknown parentage notable for its beautiful and intense orange-red foliage colour. It is relatively new, dating from 1997.

Orchidaceae (orchid family)

Hybrid Oncidium, also known as golden shower orchid, is among the hundreds of epiphytes grown on the Supertrees. Over 600 species of *Oncidium* grow in tropical American forests and thousands of artificial hybrids have been bred from them. Many, such as the ones displayed on the Supertrees, have been developed for cut flowers. These orchids are vigorous and floriferous with durable and long-lasting flowers. Displayed on and around the Supertrees are the hybrids *Oncidium* Gower Ramsey 'Golden Wish' and *Oncidium* Gower Ramsey 'Sunkist'. These plants were chosen based on their ability to flower throughout the year.

Aristolochiaceae (pipewort family)

Aristolochia leuconeura. This tropical 'pipevine', a high-climbing vine, is found in Central America and Peru. The rather small, brownish flowers are borne on its corky lower stems, but its main claim to horticultural value are its leaves, which are large, dark green with silver to gold veins.

Two 42-metre-tall Supertrees in the Supertree Grove are equipped with lifts to carry visitors up to this highlight experience. To top it off, literally, the tallest Supertree at 50 metres in height houses a treetop bistro, with panoramic views of the Gardens and the surrounding Marina Bay area. This elevated fusion of greenery and gastronomy epitomises how gardens can embrace and embellish the enjoyment of life's simplest pleasures.

> A TREETOP WALK AMONGST THE SUPERTREES IN THE SUPERTREE GROVE AWAITS AT AN AERIAL WALKWAY THAT IS 22 METRES HIGH AND 128 METRES LONG.

> ## JUST AS FASCINATING IS THE INTERFACE BETWEEN NATURE AND TECHNOLOGY IN THE PHYSICAL DIMENSION OF THE SUPERTREES.

Just as fascinating is the interface between nature and technology in the physical dimension of the Supertrees. This can be seen, for example, in the lattices of circular steel sections that weigh between 20 and 85 tonnes and make up the branches that reach right up to the tips of the Supertrees' canopies.

Where possible, aspects of nature, such as asymmetry and the prevalence of certain shapes such as rounded edges, were also mimicked as much as they are respected as design guiding principles. The vertical steel bars that reinforce the trunks are slim and lightweight to add to the Supertrees' elegant and aesthetic quality.

The way that nature is imitated is further illustrated in the technical challenges in recreating the 'anticlastic' feature of nature, that is, the way that curves relate in giving shape. For example, the shape of leaves typically includes a double curvature. Palm fronds curve in a direction opposite to the stem, and this is what holds leaves in place on branches, up against the force of gravity and winds. This principle of physics is applied to the way the steel branches at the top of each Supertree are arranged. It is actually a repeated pattern, and the apparent randomness is an illusion.

The laws of physics also demanded that the vertical planting should ideally start rising from the ground and stop at the top of the trunks, leaving the steel branches bare. This was necessary to avoid potential problems that might arise from the added weight of the plants in the event of strong winds.

The final shape of the Supertrees is another illustration of the resolution of the ongoing creative tension, and passionate debate, between the project's foreign and local consultants, and between the design engineers and the engineers who had to submit the designs for building approval. The original design intent was for the Supertrees to be as slender and shapely as the regulations would permit. This required the load distribution to be mostly vertical, carried by the steel frames that simulate the Supertrees' 'bark' and 'branches'. The opposing aim — with a greater concern for stability and erring more on the side of caution — was for more of the weight to be supported horizontally, connected to the Supertrees' inner concrete core, which would have made them chunkier.

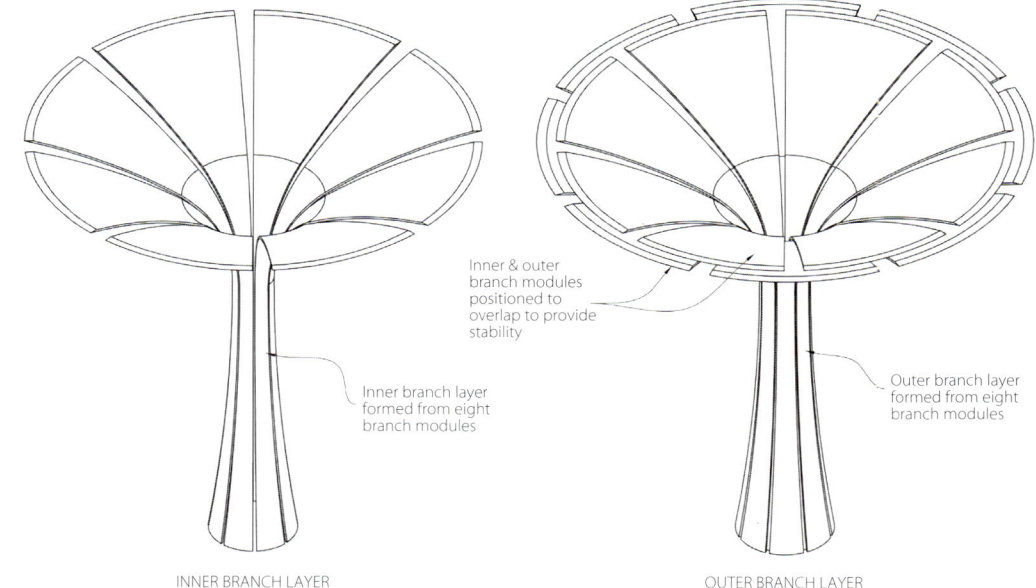

INNER BRANCH LAYER

OUTER BRANCH LAYER

Inner branch layer formed from eight branch modules

Inner & outer branch modules positioned to overlap to provide stability

Outer branch layer formed from eight branch modules

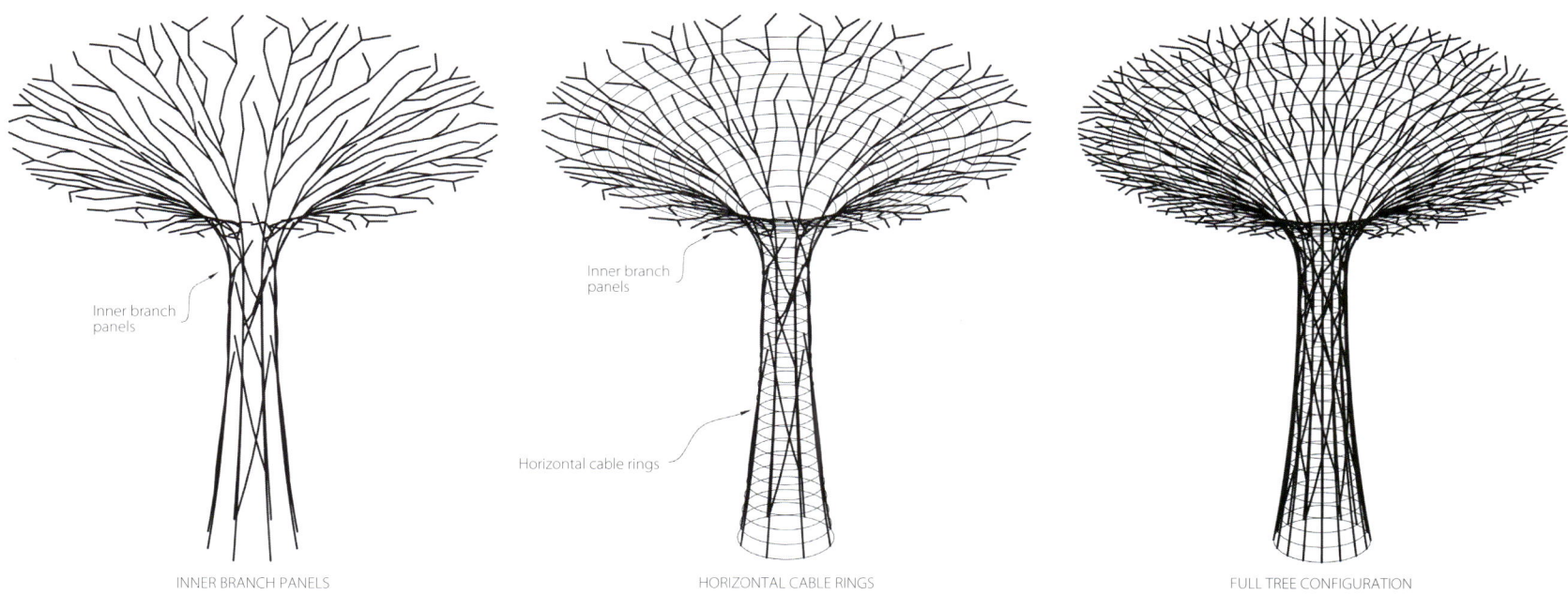

INNER BRANCH PANELS HORIZONTAL CABLE RINGS FULL TREE CONFIGURATION

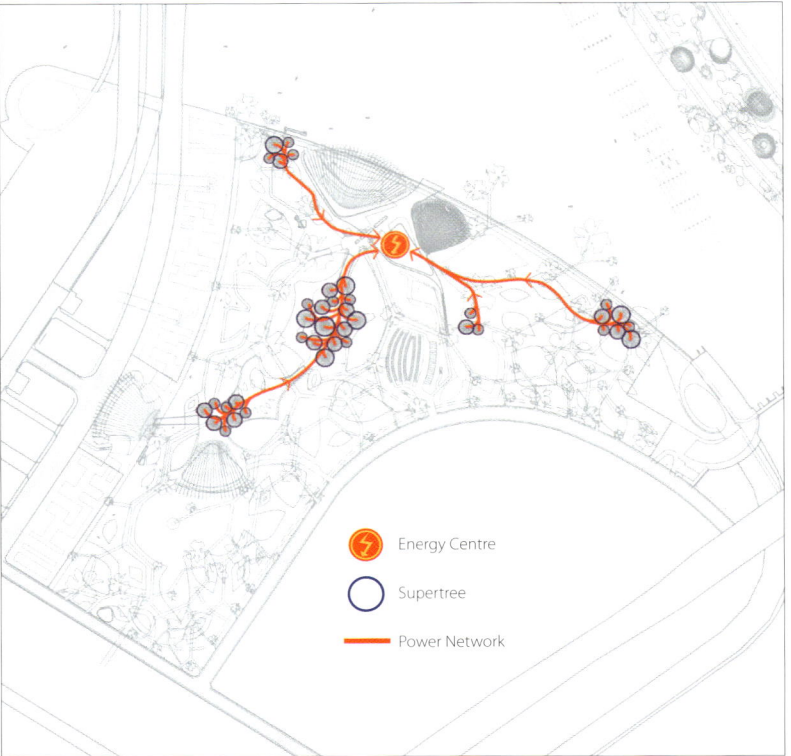

Supertree Environmental Web: POWER

Supertree Environmental Web: SITE POWER NETWORK

Pillars of sustainability

The horticultural harvest at the Supertrees is complemented by sustainable sophistication. The interplay in the Gardens between the literal and figurative, the physical and symbolic, continues with the roles that the Supertrees play in re-enacting and reflecting nature at the Gardens. There is symbolic value in the Supertrees representing the ecological cycles of nature (carbon, water, energy, nutrient and mineral), as well as in their actual functioning as sustainable energy cycles in areas such as planting, shade and maintenance — solar, biomass, water and dehumidification. Nature's balance is recreated in a few ways.

At the same time as they recreate the support structures of nature, 11 of the Supertrees have in-built features that enable them to function as environmental engines and self-sustaining systems for Gardens by the Bay. In seven of the Supertrees, the insides of their 'crowns' are equipped with photovoltaic features such as solar panels that will provide some 67 per cent of the energy required to light the trees at night. The sun's energy is harnessed also to generate electricity that powers pumps that will also draw water from underground rainwater reservoirs located within the grounds of the Gardens. This water will then be used to irrigate the trees and plants within the Gardens.

Similarly, four of the Supertrees also act as an exhaust system for the conservatories. The three Supertrees next to the Dragonfly Lake are used as chimneys to draw in warm air from the adjacent glass domes, releasing it into the atmosphere at a height, so as to help maintain the general ambient temperature of the Gardens. Another tree in the arrival cluster releases exhaust air from the turbines that generate electricity for the Gardens. In addition, in creating the water cycle of nature, an integrated irrigation system of pipes and sprinklers is built into the Supertrees to allow the plants to be bedded, irrigated, fed with liquid fertiliser and misted. The system is flexible enough to accommodate the different types of plants, ranging from the bougainvilleas and lianas for the perimeter clusters of the Supertrees to the orchids, moss and ferns for the central cluster in the Supertree Grove.

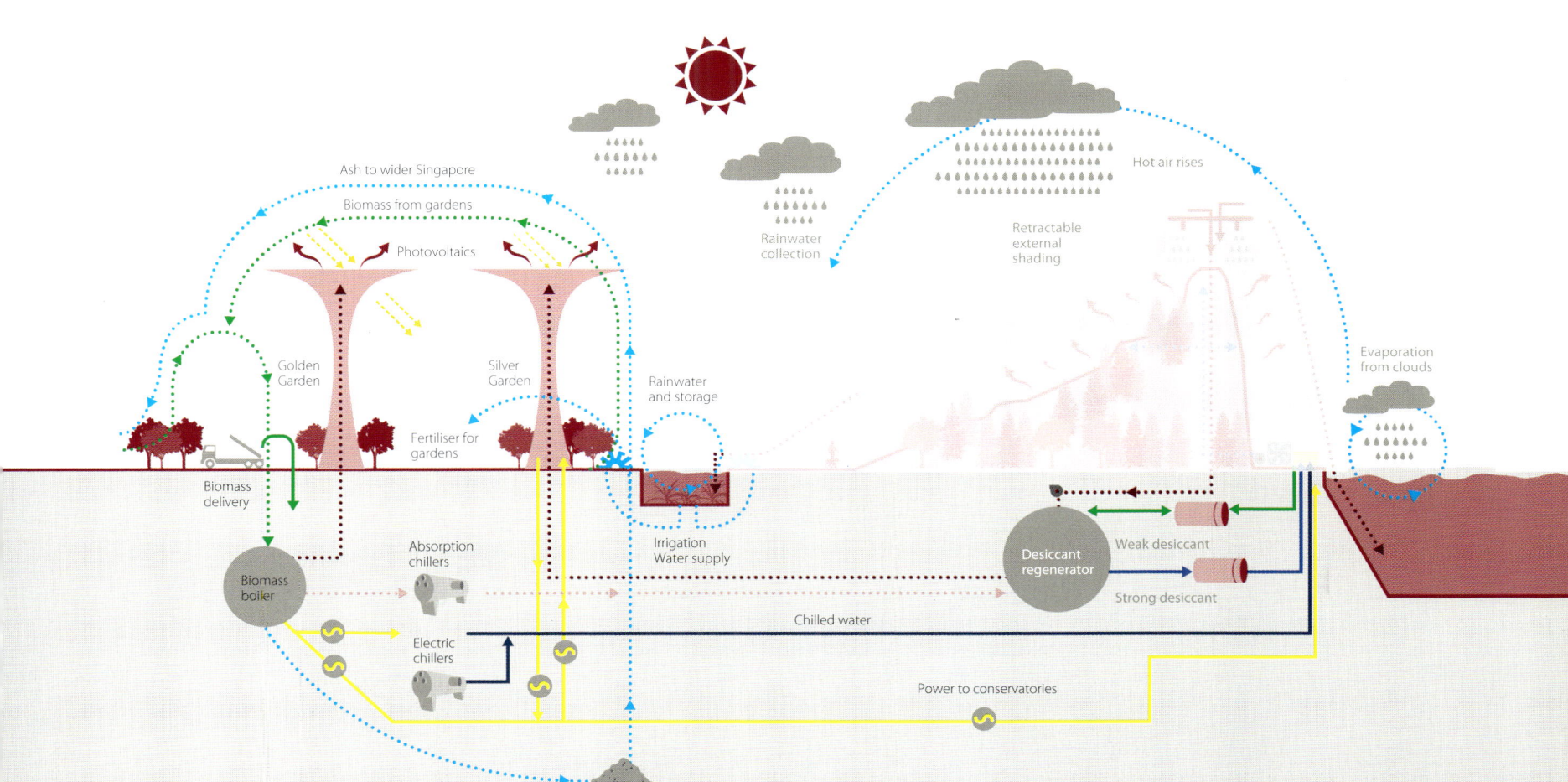

AT THE SAME TIME AS THEY RECREATE THE SUPPORT STRUCTURES OF NATURE, 11 OF THE SUPERTREES HAVE IN-BUILT FEATURES THAT ENABLE THEM TO FUNCTION AS ENVIRONMENTAL ENGINES AND SELF-SUSTAINING SYSTEMS FOR GARDENS BY THE BAY.

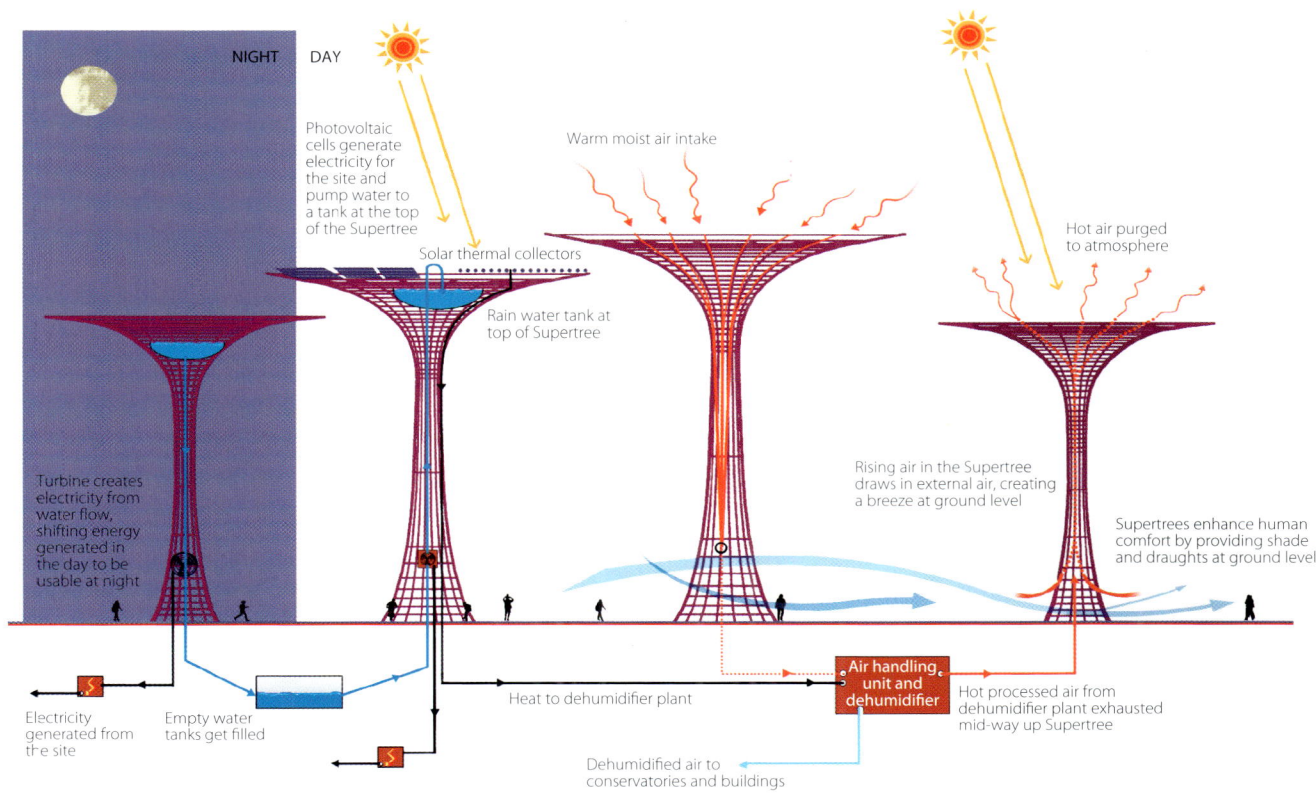
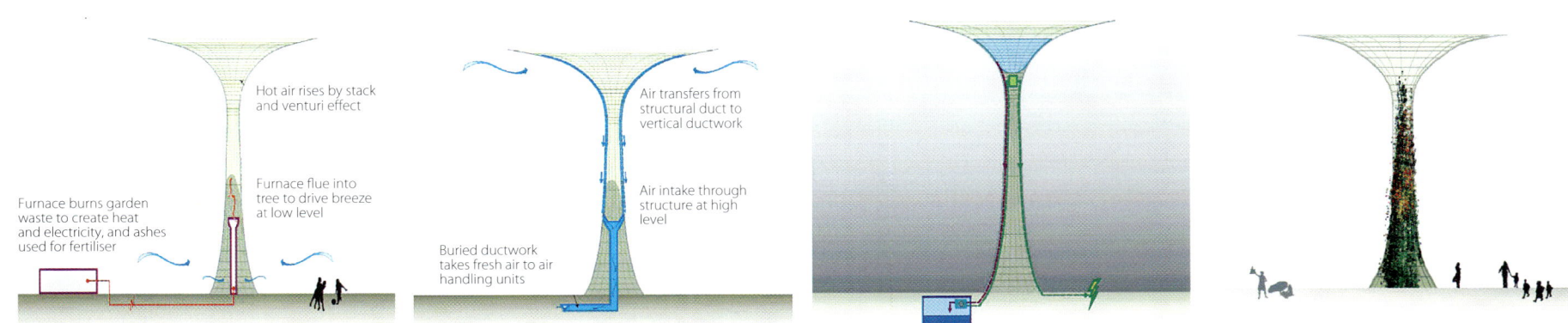

Reaching for the skies

Balance is a key aspect that is applied to the way the Supertrees were imagined in the original design. Andrew Grant of Grant Associates disclosed that the origin of the Supertrees was born of a search for balance within the whole Gardens. After the conservatories had been conceived, Grant saw the danger that the rest of the gardens could be dwarfed by the glass domes, even possibly to the extent that the surroundings would fade into obscurity. He wanted another set of structures of appreciable height and interest, "something that had complementary power and status, something of a certain scale" that would also be unique and unlike anything in the rest of the world. For him, the mental images that served as early sources of inspiration for the Supertrees were of the eucalyptus trees in the Valley of the Giants in Western Australia that can grow up to 60 metres high.

But at the same time, he did not want the Supertrees to rise taller than the conservatories, so that the Flower Dome and Cloud Forest biomes would remain the dominant features in the space of Bay South Garden as a whole.

Seen from the side elevation, the two clusters of distinctive structures would also allow for a series of unfolding views into the Gardens. Looking into the future, the Supertrees, with their accelerated mature height, will also add balance to the Gardens when seen against the high-rise developments that will come up as the rest of the Marina South area is built up.

The new vistas opened up by the height and scale of the Supertrees are another demonstration of how human ingenuity enhances nature at Gardens by the Bay. This

is best appreciated along the aerial walkway of the Supertree Grove. Grant revealed that this spatial experience was originally inspired by Princess Mononoke, a 1997 epic Japanese anime historical fantasy feature film written and directed by Hayao Miyazaki of Studio Ghibli. The story of Princess Mononoke is about the struggle between the supernatural guardians of a forest and the humans of a town who consume its resources, and explores the cyclical relationships between humans and nature.

With special lighting effects playing up the plants that wrap around the trunks, it will be almost as if life imitates art, with the Supertrees acting as a bridge between fantasy and reality.

Grant envisaged the Supertree Grove as an even more magical place at night, saturated in colour and visual spectacle. With special lighting effects playing up the plants that wrap around the trunks, it will be almost as if life imitates art, with the Supertrees acting as a bridge between fantasy and reality.

He said: "I would be very happy if observers were to associate the Gardens by the Bay with a futuristic view of the world, and see its imagery as dynamic and fantastic." This comes across through the artistry that brings to life the whole array of edutainment aspects in the Gardens. For instance, the Supertree Grove will have extensive

The shaping of
THE SUPERTREES

Grant Associates led the Gardens design team to develop the final Supertree design, using the whole array of tools available to the 21st-century designer. This was accomplished over a period of three years in four distinct phases — international competition, masterplan, advanced design development and planting design development

International competition (2006)
The basic form and concept of the Supertrees — to act as visual magnets and environmental engines for the gardens and cooled conservatories — was developed at the international masterplan competition stage in 2006. The primary design tools used at this stage were hand sketches with simple form-finding computer and photoshop modelling culminating in the winning concept.

Masterplan (2007)
The composition of the Supertrees was developed in parallel with the evolving garden design during the masterplan stage. The heights of the structures were refined and the concept of an aerial walkway enclosing half of the Supertree Grove was investigated. In addition to hand sketches, increasingly sophisticated computer-modelling techniques were used to develop options for the physical form of the Supertrees and determine optimum structural design solutions. Three-dimensional (3D) computer-aided design (CAD) software was used by Grant Associates to develop physical forms inspired by nature, which also help to reinforce and make reference to the visual language being developed concurrently throughout the gardens. Structural engineers Atelier One imported Grant Associates' 3D CAD model into their own structural analysis software and developed the geometry to arrive at a graceful and efficient structural solution. The results of the structural analysis were then fed into the architects' model and the process repeated until all parties were satisfied that the optimum solution had been achieved.

Advanced design development (2008)
During the advanced design development stage, the heights of the Supertrees were established so that the design of the concrete core and the steelwork could be finalised. The inner concrete core, the profile of the Supertrees and the Supertrees' primary structure were also fixed.

The primary structure of each Supertree consists of 16 steel tubes arranged radially into eight inner members and eight outer members tied together by clamped circumferential cables to form a tensioned net. A tensioned net structure is inherently strong with vertical tube members and horizontal cables acting as a single surface that is structurally efficient. This sophisticated structural solution allowed the design team, working with local engineers Meinhardt Infrastructure, to keep the diameter of the steel tubes as narrow as possible to create the most elegant and materially efficient structure. With the primary structural strategy fixed, the team then developed the branch layout to create the structure that is visible today.

Three distinct steel layout options were selected from numerous models for 3D printing — faceted random branch layout, geometric hexagonal surface and free-form double curved branch layout. For each option, 3D printers used a computer model to create a three-dimensional physical model through a process called selective laser sintering. Here, a powdered nylon material was heated together until the branch layout solidified, replicating the 3D computer model. When the printed 3D models were reviewed, it was decided that the faceted random branch layout provided the optimal structure and the best visual fit within the language of the entire gardens. This model was then refined to create the final branch layout, which appears as random, but is actually fabricated from eight identical repeating segments or 'leaves' to simplify the fabrication and erection processes. The final design was issued to the contractors as a series of detailed 2D drawings extracted from a 3D model.

As the design of the Supertrees progressed, the aerial walkway was developed further. The result is a curved 128-metre-long walkway, swooping around the eastern side of the Supertree Grove. Suspended 22 metres above the gardens below, it connects two 42-metre-tall Supertrees. In order to create the best possible visitor experience and offer unimpeded views, the team selected the most technically challenging option — suspending the walkway from the steel branches of five adjacent Supertrees.

Engineers from Atelier One studied Grant Associates' 3D CAD model to analyse the optimum design solution for the aerial walkway. The final solution was a steel tube, 139.7 millimetres in diameter, which flanks the length of the walkway. The tubes are securely connected to two adjacent Supertrees at various points by 265 stainless steel cables, each 12 millimetres thick. Due to the complex geometries involved in each walkway hanger, every one of the 530 cable connections is geometrically unique to avoid components clashing with one another. A deck securely attached to the steel tubes provides the surface for visitors to walk on. A lightweight handrail and balustrade completes the walkway. The lightweight design and materials serve a purpose — they provide visitors with the sensation of floating above the gardens and through a unique forest canopy.

Planting design development (2009 onwards)

For Grant Associates and local landscape contractor Tropical Environment, the key challenge with housing the plants was to create a low-maintenance, cost-effective substrate that would provide a base for a lush, seamless, vertical garden. The plan was for dense vegetation to cover the steel structure upwards from the base of the Supertree, dispersing at the 'throat' (where the trunk meets the branches) to maintain the lightweight filigree of the canopy branch structure. In order to achieve this effect, the designers worked closely with the National Parks Board's horticultural team to develop the planting schedule, which would detail the species and size of the plants to be used.

Two types of planting systems are used to clad the Supertrees. One is a rigid 'pillow', or base, filled with a lightweight planting medium; the second is a steel mesh panel to which plants are simply clipped. Beyond the throat level, climbers — planted at the base and trained by wires along the skin — will grow into the lower tree canopy. One of the key technical challenges was to create a growing media in a panelised form that would allow single panels to be removed individually to allow for variation in the planting mix and to create spectacular displays to mark specific events or a particular time of the year.

As for irrigation, a drip feed system to water the plants is supplemented by a series of pop-up sprinklers designed to simulate rainfall. Both systems are linked in to the garden-wide information technology control system which uses weather and moisture sensors to determine when the irrigation systems need to be activated.

With a little bit of help from man, the Supertrees give the bromeliads and other plants an environment as conducive as, if not more so than, any found in nature.

> THERE IS SYMBOLIC VALUE IN THE SUPERTREES REPRESENTING THE ECOLOGICAL CYCLES OF NATURE (CARBON, WATER, ENERGY, NUTRIENT AND MINERAL), AS WELL AS IN THEIR ACTUAL FUNCTIONING AS SUSTAINABLE ENERGY CYCLES.

5
Themed Gardens
Nature's Bounty

The themed gardens present their stories in clustered displays arranged along two main narrative threads: 'Plants and Planet' and 'Plants and People'.

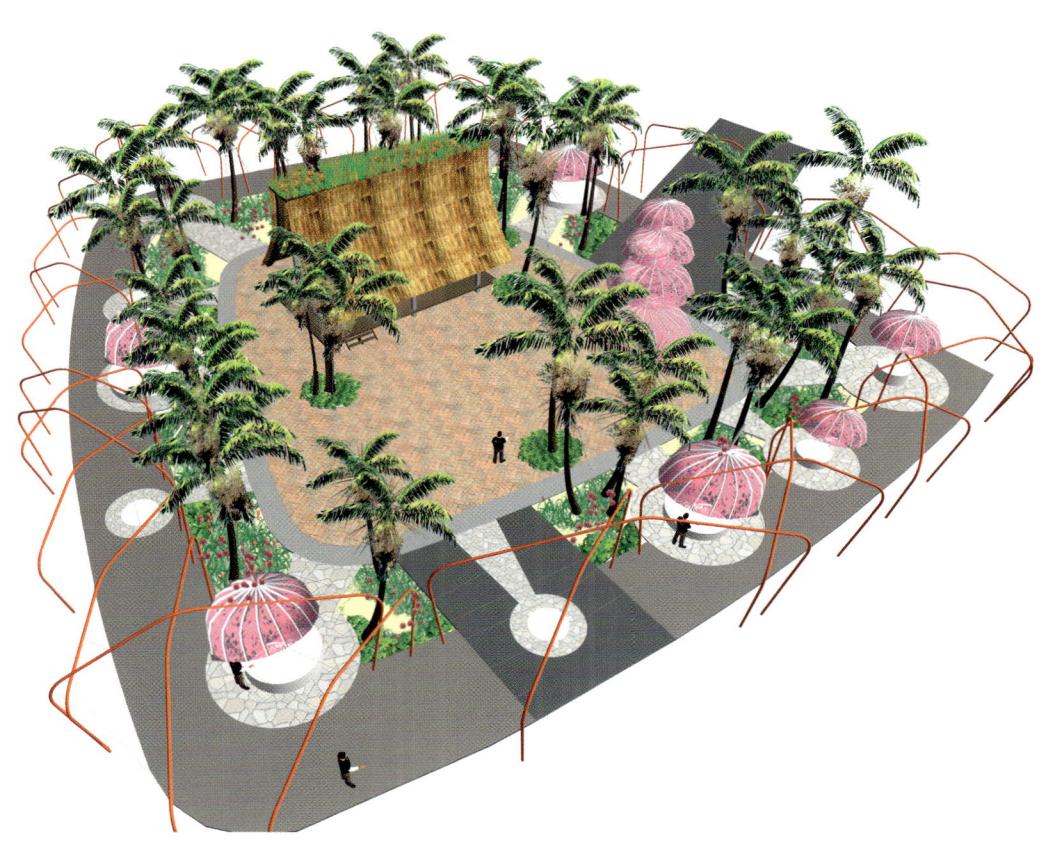

The themed gardens present their stories in clustered displays arranged along two main narrative threads — 'Plants and Planet', which extends in its layout into the Cloud Forest, the cool-moist conservatory; and 'Plants and People', which runs along a ridge into the Flower Dome, the cool-dry conservatory.

Whereas the conservatories and Supertrees draw the eye to the skies, arresting attention with their height and scale, the themed gardens of Gardens by the Bay are more firmly grounded, taking visitors to different dimensions of discovery and delight.

Highlighting various aspects of how plants relate to the rest of the biosphere, these gardens venture deep into the world of plants, steeped in their ecological, biological, cultural, sociological and economic milieus. These presentations of key aspects of plants branch out to embrace their global context, even as they are also rooted in the history and culture of Singapore and Southeast Asia. Here, in more ways than one, nestles the heart of Gardens by the Bay.

PLANTS AND

> 'PLANTS AND PLANET' HIGHLIGHTS THE ABILITY OF LIVING ORGANISMS IN NATURE TO ADAPT TO PARTICULAR ENVIRONMENTS AND THE BIODIVERSITY OF PLANT LIFE ON THE PLANET WITH A PARTICULAR FOCUS ON RAINFOREST SPECIES. THERE ARE SIX THEMED GARDENS WITHIN THIS SECTION, NAMED 'WORLD OF PLANTS'.

The Secret Life of Trees

This garden showcases all aspects of trees — examining the details of their form, including the different components of trunks, bark, wood and canopies, as well as aspects such as leaves and photosynthesis, roots and their relationship with anchorage, nutrients and moisture. Also explored are the functions of trees, especially in a rainforest.

The World of Palms

This garden celebrates the rich diversity of palms from the rainforest and their particular niches in the ecology of trees. Different types of fronds, fruits and seeds are highlighted, as are the versatile uses of these plants, for example, for making building materials such as thatch and raffia cord, and as an extremely important source of food.

PLANET

The Understorey

This garden digs deep to explore life in the forest below the canopy, illuminating how plants have adapted to environments with perpetual low-light conditions and nutrient-deficient soil. The cycle of decomposition in this complex ecosystem is also featured, as well as how some plants protect themselves against predators, just as animals do in the animal kingdom.

Awesome Fruits and Flowers

This garden harvests the most interesting information about flowers and fruits — their lifespan, form and function, dispersal and reproduction, as well as the domestication of rainforest fruits and their wild relatives. Plant adaptation is highlighted, including how blossoms are shaped to attract specific pollinators for the perpetuation of plant species, and how they sometimes mimic other facets of nature to achieve this aim. A central feature of this garden is the cannonball tree with its impressive fruit.

Discovery

This garden looks at plant evolution throughout the lifespan of planet Earth, and focuses on ancient plant groups such as cycads and conifers. It explains how through co-evolution between plants and insects, flowering plants arrived to the breathtaking diversity observed today. By providing the visitor with a glimpse of the very long time it took to arrive at the plant diversity seen today, it also draws a comparison with the accelerated rate of extinction caused by man.

Web of Life

This garden looks at the inter-relationship between flora and fauna, such as hornbills, as well as the food chains in the rainforest. The keystone plants in this garden are different species of fig belonging to the genus Ficus, which comprises over 1,000 species worldwide. Species of Ficus provide a bounty of fruit and feed many species of rainforest animals. Keystone species are vital to hold habitats together, and their destruction, whether through climate change or human activity, affects the ecosystem. The central features here are the topiary animal artworks in the style of American artist Jeff Koons. These topiaries are made of a species of fig known as Indian laurel or curtain fig (*Ficus microcarpa*).

Swiss cheese plant

Ficus deltoidea

Cannonball tree

Cannonball tree flower

Peacock fern

Elephant fern

Elephant fern

Ficus auriculata

PLANTS AND

[CITED WITHIN THE 'PLANTS AND PEOPLE' SECTION ARE THE 'HEIRLOOM' HERITAGE GARDENS OF SINGAPORE'S PIONEER ETHNIC GROUPS WHO WERE THE COUNTRY'S INDIGENOUS AND EARLY IMMIGRANT PEOPLES.

Heritage Gardens

Distinguishing each garden is an exposition of each of the cultural groups — presented in Indian, Chinese, Malay and Colonial gardens — showcasing the plant materials they brought with them, and their subsequent influences on Singaporean culture. These gardens will feature the best of tropical horticulture and garden artistry, with mass displays of tropical flowers and brilliant foliage.

Much care was taken to create the setting for the themed gardens, revealed Andrew Grant of Grant Associates. Overall, the desired feel was not minimalist but 'intricate Asian' in aspects like the rich palette of hues such as aubergine that is created with the flowers and plants, and with complementary details such as the signage and other man-made features. The graphic designers visited parts of Singapore with strong cultural influences to acquire a feel and sense of the appropriate colour and sensory experience that the themed gardens should have.

The main colour scheme takes its hues from the local rainforest fruit, the mangosteen, with its shades of purple, red and white. Just as in the forest, where the mangosteen and its strong colours act as a kind of navigation system for birds and animals, in these themed gardens these colours signpost directions for forays of discovery into annotated stories about wide-ranging topics including the energy cycle, water cycle, biodiversity, ethnobotany and horticultural excellence.

PEOPLE

The Indian Garden

Plants pervade the spiritual and material culture of India, and a central theme in the Indian Garden is that of devotion, as expressed in plants. Plant use permeates every aspect of daily Indian life, including their use for food and for religious rituals.

Night Life of Trees motif

Terracotta horse

Featured in this garden is the banyan tree (*Ficus benghalensis*), India's national tree and an example of a culturally significant plant to the Indian community, most of whom are descended from early immigrants from South India, especially Tamil Nadu.

The garden's main design motif is inspired by *kolam*, a folk art mainly practised by women. It is a floor design in a three-dimensional image, traditionally made with rice powder and layers of flowers, lentils or unhusked rice. The 'Sacred Groves' garden highlights how, in Indian culture, certain tracts of forests are believed to be the domain of deities and gods. Some have presiding deities to whom offerings are made, and they have become ecologically important over time as a last refuge for endemic and endangered plants.

Unusual plants of the Indian Garden

Ficus religiosa, or sacred fig, peepul tree, bodhi tree
Of the Moraceae (fig family) and native to India and Indochina, this semi-deciduous tree can grow up to 35 metres tall. It is of religious significance to Buddhists, who believe that Buddha attained enlightenment beneath a bodhi tree. Its leaves, seeds, bark and fruits are found to have medicinal purposes. Its fruits are consumed to treat asthma, and its bark used to treat gonorrhoea.

Ficus benghalensis, or banyan tree
Also of the Moraceae, the banyan is the national tree of India and has a complex tangled structure of roots and branches. The name banyan means 'trader' in the Gujarati language and is derived from Banias or Indian merchants who rested under it to discuss business strategies. In Hindu mythology, Lord Shiva, the God of Health, is sometimes depicted sitting under this tree. The Great Banyan in the Kolkata Botanic Gardens is considered the widest tree in the world.

Aegle marmelos, or bael fruit
Of the Rutaceae (citrus family) and native to the Himalayas, India and Myanmar, the bael fruit is a small, deciduous, fruiting tree that grows up to 13 metres tall and provides nectar for bees. A sacred tree to Hindus, its leaves are traditionally used as offerings to Lord Shiva. The essential oil extracted from the rind is used in making perfume and soap. A ripe fruit is considered to have a tonic effect and is used particularly as a laxative. In some areas, the unripe fruit can be used to treat dysentery, haemorrhoids or diarrhoea.

Azadirachta indica, or neem tree
Of the Meliaceae (mahogany family) and native to India, Indonesia, Malaysia, Myanmar, Pakistan, Senegal, Sri Lanka and Thailand, this evergreen tree can grow up to 16 metres. It serves as a biological insect controller, source of bee nectar, and food for bats and birds. Extracts of the tree cause insects to be sterile, and the seeds provide azadirachtin, a chemical compound which disrupts the metamorphosis of insects. Non-toxic to humans, azadirachtin can destroy bacteria and over 200 insect species. The aromatic oil extracted from seeds (Margosa oil) has been used to relieve leprosy and shows anti-carcinogenic properties.

Moringa oleifera, or horseradish tree
Of the Moringaceae (horseradish tree family) and native to India, Malaysia, Oman, Qatar, Saudi Arabia, United Arab Emirates and Yemen, the horseradish tree is a fast-growing, long-lived tree that can grow up to 10 metres. Widely planted for ornamental purposes, it is an important source of bee nectar. Almost all parts of the horseradish tree are edible. Flowers are added to stews, leaves are eaten as spinach or salad. Young pods are used raw or boiled. The oily, dried, winged seeds yield important edible oil known as Ben oil, commonly used in perfumery and cosmetics, soap and machine oils, and as a salad oil.

Banyan tree

Horseradish tree

Neem tree

The Chinese Garden

This garden offers representations of the largest of Singapore's three main ethnic communities, the Chinese, who hailed mostly from the southern provinces of China, and are defined by dialect groups including Hokkien, Teochew, Hakka, Hainanese and Cantonese.

The key theme of this garden is a reflection of literature. The close relationship between scholarship and gardens is captured in the 'Four Gentlemen of Flowers' — the orchid (representing spring), bamboo (summer), chrysanthemum (autumn) and plum (winter). Writings such as the essay *Yangzhu Ji* (On Cultivating Bamboo) by the famous Tang dynasty poet Bai Juyi extol the characteristics of the bamboo in providing *junzi* (morally superior men) with reminders of proper conduct. The 'Four Gentlemen of Flowers' also form a painting genre on its own, with elaborate symbolism for each plant.

Ancient Chinese garden culture is closely aligned with nature, emphasising balance and harmony through imitating nature using water features, rocks and pruned plants. One of the clearest differences between a Chinese garden and a Western garden is summarised by the idea that in the West, a garden is planted, but a Chinese garden is built. Rather than flowers, trees and shrubs, the most striking features of a Chinese garden are its streams, rockeries and structures such as pagodas or pavilions.

The Chinese word for landscape is *shanshui* — literally, 'mountain, water' — and, just as these shapes of nature are in free form, the central intention behind the Chinese garden is to simulate nature in all its irregularity and disorder. The philosophical basis for this is the Chinese (or Taoist-influenced) belief that man should always aim to live in harmony with nature rather than impose himself on it. The architecture in a Chinese garden can be playful and metaphorical in the use and positioning of elements such as plants and rocks, aligned as it is with the close relationship between gardens and poetry in Chinese history. Gateways are circular and metaphorically called 'moon gates', differentiating them from the traditional entrances of homes or buildings, which have regular doors.

In creating a Chinese garden in tropical Singapore, some of the major symbolic plants that would only thrive in temperate climes had to be replaced. For instance, the plum, almond and cherry blossom (*Prunus* spp.) had to be substituted by the Bao Fan Flower (*Lagoerstremia* spp.) and Kayu Arang (*Cratoxylon* spp.), the weeping willow is represented by the Australian weeping tea tree, while the flexible leaves of the temperate poplar (*Populus* spp.) are emulated by the Chinese tallow tree (*Triadica sebifera*) from farther south.

Natural stone in the Chinese Garden

White mulberry

Toog trees in the Chinese garden, which is home for old, gnarled specimen trees

Unusual plants of the Chinese Garden

Morus alba, or white mulberry/silkworm mulberry
Of the Moraceae (fig family) and native to central and northern China, this is a short-lived, fast-growing, small to medium-sized tree which grows up to 8 metres tall. It is an excellent animal feed for livestock, and the leaves are the main food for silkworms. The bark fibre is used to make textile and paper, and the fruit is also eaten, often dried or made into wine. In traditional Chinese medicine, the fruit can inhibit premature greying of hair, improve digestion, stimulate the appetite, promote gastric juice secretion, and treat constipation, chronic gastritis and hepatitis.

Osmanthus fragrans, or *gui hua*, sweet osmanthus, tea olive, sweet olive
Of the Oleaceae (olive family), this is a native of parts of Asia from the Himalayas east through southern China (Guizhou, Sichuan, Yunnan) to Taiwan and southern Japan. It is known as the City Flower for Hangzhou, China. A shrub or small tree up to 12 metres tall, it is appreciated for its clusters of very fragrant white and pale yellow flowers. The fruit is fleshy with a single hard-shelled seed. The fragrant flowers are infused with tea leaves to produce the scented *gui hua* Chinese tea, or used to make jam, desserts and liquor.

Cratoxylon formosum, or Pink mempat
Of the Hypericaceae (St John wort's family), this is a native of Indochina, Malaysia and Philippines. *Cratoxylon*, in Greek, means 'hard wood', while *formosum* means 'beautiful', of a fine and delicate appearance, in Latin. The wood is very hard and durable, and can be used for construction and furniture. In Thailand, the young leaves are collected and eaten as a raw vegetable.

Juniperus chinensis, or Chinese juniper
Of the Cupressaceae (cypress family) and native to Northeast Asia, China, Mongolia, Japan, Korea and the southeast of Russia, *Juniperus chinensis* has two types of leaves — young (needle-like) and adult (scale-like). This ornamental landscape plant is a popular species for bonsai. A juniper bonsai symbolises longevity, strength, athleticism and fertility.

The Malay Garden

The Malay Garden recalls the culture of the indigenous people of Singapore who originally hailed also from Malaysia, Indonesia, Brunei and Philippines.

The garden's theme revolves around life in a *kampong* (Malay for 'village'), with its structures made of timber, attap and other plant items. Inspiration is drawn from places such as the Royal Garden on Bukit Larangan (today's Fort Canning Hill), with representations of the cultural significance of key plants, poetry and proverbs related to plants, and a video featuring crafts such as pandan leaf weaving and wood carving.

The cultural significance of plants figures in the many place names associated with Malay plant names. In Singapore, the name Changi may have been derived from the climbing shrub that grew in the area, Changi Ular (*Apama corymbosa*) or the local timber named Chengal (*Neobalanocarpus heimii*). The name Kampong Glam (Glam Village) could refer to the Gelam tree (*Melaleuca cajuputi* or *Melaluca leucadendron*), which once grew in abundance in the area but is no longer found in the wild. This settlement of Kampong Glam is older than modern Singapore, being already in existence at the time of Sir Stamford Raffles' arrival in 1819. The area is significant also in Singapore's history, as it became the historic seat of Malay royalty when the British installed Tengku Hussein as the Sultan of Johore in February 1819. Sultan Hussein built his new palace and mosque at Kampong Glam.

Belimbing flower

Belimbing fruit

Tongkat Ali

Breadfruit tree

Jambu Air flower

Jambu Air fruit

Breadfruit

Unusual plants of the Malay Garden

Averrhoa bilimbi, or Belimbing

Of the Oxalidaceae (starfruit family), this tree hails originally from the Moluccas Islands in Indonesia but is now cultivated throughout the country. Also known as cucumber tree, it is a slow-growing, interesting tree that flowers and fruits from its main stem rather than through new shoots. Its flowers are borne directly on the trunk and, when fruiting, the tree may be totally covered in cucumber-shaped green fruits. Its leaves are used against infections, inflammations and rheumatism, and its flowers are used to make a syrup to relieve coughs.

Artocarpus altilis, or breadfruit

Of the Moraceae (fig family), this tree with beautiful, feather-shaped leaves is originally from Southeast Asia but nowadays cultivated in many tropical countries. The fruits of this seedless plant can be used as a bread substitute, by baking, roasting or boiling its flesh — hence its name. The 18th-century British naval officer Captain William Bligh (who travelled with the voyager James Cook on his journeys) introduced this plant species to Jamaica in 1793, aiming to provide inexpensive food for slaves.

Eurycoma longifolia, or Tongkat Ali

Of the Simaroubaceae (bitterwood family), this unbranched treelet can grow to 15 metres tall and is native to Malaysia and Indonesia. Its extremely bitter leaves, bark and roots are traditionally used for its anti-malarial, aphrodisiac, anti-diabetic and anti-microbial effects, and also as fish-poison. Recently, it has become a very sought-after medicine for male 'vitality', being referred to as Malaysia's 'homegrown Viagra'.

Areca catechu, or betel nut palm

Of the Arecaceae (palm family), this is an elegant palm with golden-yellow fruits. This species is native to the Philippines but widely cultivated in Southeast Asia and elsewhere. The dried nuts, together with betel leaves (Piper betle, Uncaria gambir) are used to prepare betel quiffs that are chewed as a mild stimulant. Chewing betel was a popular practice among Peranakan women, and elaborate betel sets played an important role as part of wedding ceremonies that lasted several days.

Syzygium samarangense, or Jambu Air

Of the Myrtaceae (gum tree family), this treelet has large, rigid leaves and beautiful shaving brush-like flowers, followed by porcelain-pink to red fruits. It is native to Bangladesh and the Solomon Islands but widely introduced to many tropical countries. Its attractive flowers with many stamens are pollinated by bees, while its fruits apparently rely on fruit bats for their dispersal. Its astringent flowers are mildly antibiotic, and can be employed to treat fevers and diarrhoea.

The Colonial Garden

The exploration of the interface between plants and human culture continues in the Colonial Garden.

Here, the central theme is a reflection of strategic ambition, as represented by Singapore as a vital entrepot port along the main sea routes between China and India, with international trade as the focus of a bright economic future.

During the colonial era, Singapore became a major centre of re-export, including for plant products. Though trade as a whole was the ultimate factor that underpinned the British founding of Singapore, plants came to play an important part in the city-state's early history due to Raffles' belief that cash crops could be established here and the importance he placed on agricultural research. It is telling that one of the first things Raffles did was to establish the experimental spice garden on Government Hill, or Fort Canning Hill as it is known today.

Colonial botanic gardens, with their orderly landscapes, were used as experimental plots to test and cultivate potentially economically lucrative crops, fruits, spices and other plants. These plants brought economic benefit to the British Empire and helped spur further imperial expansion, with Kew Gardens in London acting as a storehouse for the worldwide exchange of plants.

The main themes of the Colonial Garden centre on the discovery and commercial exploitation of useful plants such as nutmeg, pepper, clove and rubber. Early European investments in crops included nutmeg, coffee, coconut, sugar, cotton, cinnamon, clove and indigo, but almost all of them proved disastrous, ultimately failing. Plantations of nutmeg thrived for a period, but disease struck and destroyed all the nutmeg plantations in the 1860s.

The importance of Singapore on the Spice Route is emphasised by showing how the spice trade had a direct impact on the founding of Singapore in 1819. Raffles' choice in establishing a trading post in Singapore was in large part due to the British desire to break Dutch monopoly over trade in the region. In the 1840s, the colonial government hoped that Singapore could become a major exporter of spices, palm oil and coconut, and hundreds of acres of land were offered to ambitious Europeans for the development of plantations.

This section also features the black-and-white houses that are unique to the region. They reflect the island's colonial past and encapsulate the quintessence of that bygone era, recalling lives of ease and elegance. An example of a colonial street name with an interesting history is D'Almeida Street, named after Dr Sir Jose D'Almeida Carvalho e Silva (1784–1850), who came to Singapore in 1825. He was very keen on agriculture and was one of the founding members of the Agricultural and Horticultural Society in 1836. He owned a large plantation called Bandula near Serangoon Road where he grew coffee, coconut, cotton and nutmeg.

Unusual plants of the Colonial Garden

Syzygium aromaticum, or clove

Of the Myrtaceae (gum tree family), this is a small, slow-growing tree originally from the Moluccas Islands of Indonesia. It is the source of the highly-prized spice known as clove. The unopened, cream-and-pink flower buds are harvested by hand and dried in the sun until they become reddish-brown. Initially used as a medicinal plant by the Chinese and Egyptians, cloves were taken to Europe by Arab traders and became a very highly prized commodity in the 15th century, serving a variety of medicinal and culinary purposes. Nowadays, the crop is grown mostly in Madagascar, Zanzibar and Indonesia.

Hevea brasiliensis, or rubber tree

Of the Euphorbiaceae (spurge family), this tall tree native from western Amazonia has tri-foliolate leaves and large fruits bearing three mottled seeds. All parts of the plant have latex, which is harvested from cuts made in its trunk and converted into rubber. Initially, production of rubber was a monopoly in Brazil, but in 1876 the British obtained 70,000 seeds and sent them to Kew Gardens where less than 3,000 germinated. The seedlings were carefully packed in miniature greenhouses known as wardian cases and sent to the Botanic Gardens in Singapore, where Sir Henry Ridley, also known as 'Mad' and 'Rubber Ridley', was responsible for its propagation and extensive introduction into other British colonies.

Elaeis guineensis, or oil palm

Of the Arecaceae (palm family), this oil palm is originally from West Africa, but nowadays is cultivated in many tropical regions of the world. It was introduced by the British to Malaysia in 1910 and subsequently substituted for rubber as the demand for its cheap, saturated oil increased worldwide. There are two types of oil produced from its fruit — one pressed from the red, meaty outside of the fruit, mostly for culinary use, and one obtained from the kernel, used in food industry and as bio-fuel.

Clove

Oil palm

Allspice

Frangipani

Cananga odorata, or *ylang ylang*

Of the Annonaceae (soursop family), this is a medium-sized, evergreen tree, with large leaves distributed evenly in the branches and obscuring beautiful, cream-yellow hanging flowers with six long, curly petals, followed by green clusters of fruit. The flowers of this species are used to produce a high-quality essential oil used in the perfume, cosmetic and aromatherapy industries. Originally from India, Southeast Asia and Australia, this species is now cultivated mostly in Madagascar and other islands off the East African coast.

SOME SCULPTURES
in the themed gardens

Li Xiang

Lion sculpture

Wooden crocodile with young

Li Xiang (离乡)
Located at the Chinese Garden, Li Xiang (离乡) is a two-piece sculpture from Xiamen, China. The first piece is a block of springstone with an empty space in the form of a human shape. The second piece is the 'missing' human from the first piece, placed some 10 metres away. Li Xiang represents a man leaving his country, a reference to the early Chinese immigrants from various provinces in China who came to Singapore in search of a better life.

Lion sculpture
Located at the Baobab Village inside the Flower Dome conservatory, this lion sculpture carved from springstone is a fine example of the strong culture of stone carving in Zimbabwe (widely known as Shona Sculpture). It was displayed at the Kirstenbosch National Botanical Garden in South Africa, nestled at the foot of Table Mountain in Cape Town. The garden regularly features Zimbabwean stone sculptures associated with the Chapungu Sculpture Park in Zimbabwe.

Wooden crocodile with young
This gigantic crocodile was carved by a Timorese sculptor. The intricate artwork was painstakingly carved with many baby crocodiles on its surface, creating an awesome sight at the staircase outdoors at The Canopy, the plaza between the two conservatories.

Wooden eagle

Buddha under the Bodhi tree

Wooden leopard and tiger

Wooden eagle
This eagle sculpture was carved from a lychee tree (*Litchi chinensis*, from the longan family — Sapindaceae). While the pedestal was made from an untreated tree trunk, the artist's great mastery was employed in using the intricate filigrane pattern of the roots for making the bird's wings, while a more solid piece was carved into the head and impressive talons. Located at the end of the Baobab Village overlooking the Flower Field inside the Flower Dome, this majestic eagle from Shandong, China is commanding and graceful at the same time.

Buddha under the Bodhi tree
This stone sculpture of the benevolent Buddha, placed under a bodhi tree at the Heritage Gardens, is by sculptor Wang Rong Hai (王荣海), from Xiamen, China. As visitors walk from the Indian Garden to the Chinese Garden and chance upon this sculpture, the artwork's strategic location reminds them of how Buddhism travelled from India to China some 2,000 years ago.

Wooden leopard and tiger
Located outdoors at The Canopy, these leopard and tiger figures were carved from recycled Khaya wood (*Khaya senegalensis*, from the mahogany family — Meliaceae). Designed by Singaporean artist Eng Siak Loy, these artworks further jazz up a viewing deck overlooking Marina Bay, and also serve as seats for garden visitors.

6
Lakes and Main Gardens
Clean Waters, Fragile Forest

Around the cooled conservatories, Supertrees and themed gardens, the rest of the Gardens at Bay South reveal — at once — the vulnerability and resilience of nature.

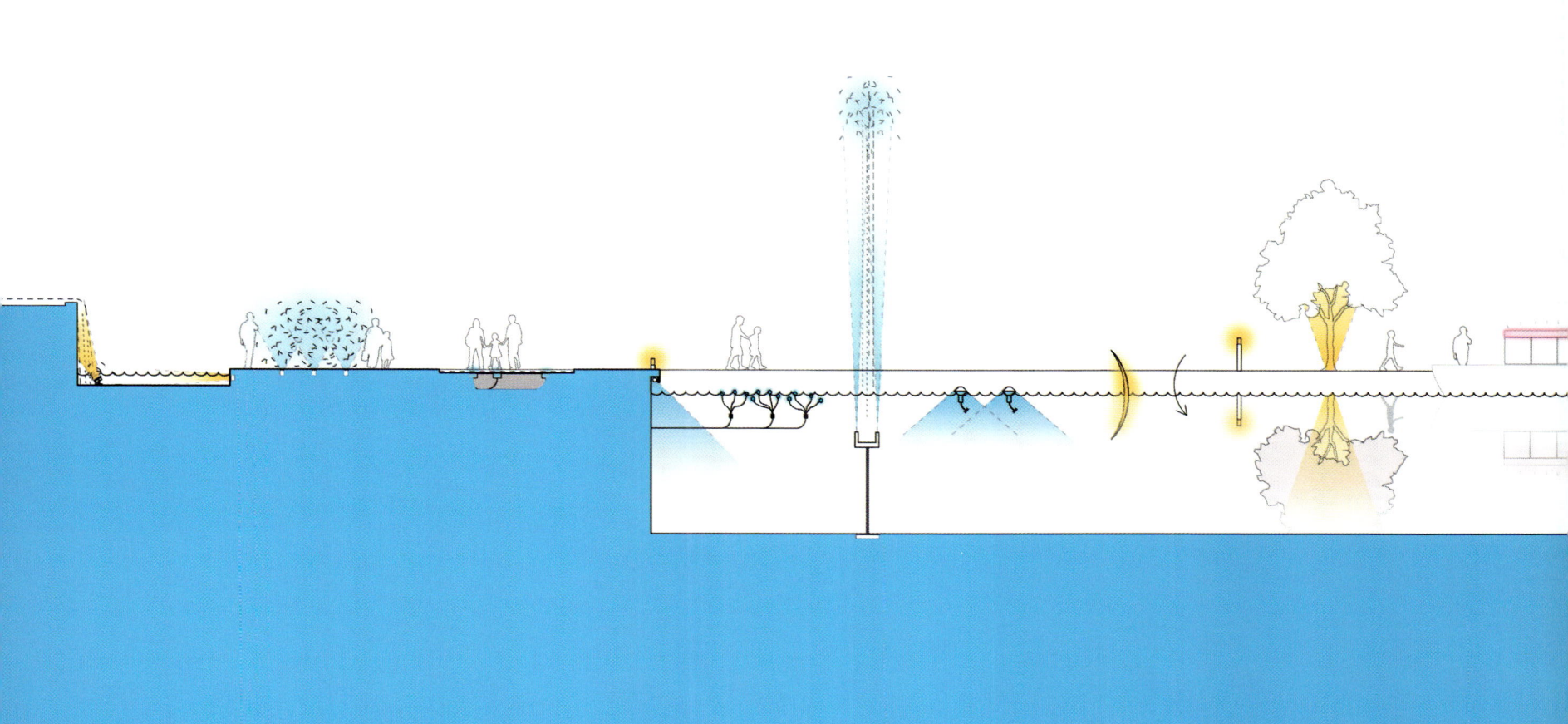

DISPLAYS AND PLANTINGS OF THE SPLENDOUR OF A VULNERABLE EARTH ARE INTERWOVEN WITH THE GARDENS' SYSTEM OF ELONGATED LAKES TO HIGHLIGHT THE FLOW OF WATER BETWEEN THE MAN-MADE WATER BODIES AMIDST A NETWORK OF INVITING AND INFORMATIVE TRAILS AND OTHER AMENITIES.

THE VITAL IMPORTANCE OF SUSTAINABILITY AND SURVIVAL IS EMPHASISED, EVEN AS NATURE'S INGENUITY IN SELF-SUSTENANCE BECOMES PLAIN TO SEE.

THE LAKES

Going with the flow

The Gardens' system of interconnected lakes, which spans roughly 5 hectares in surface area and stretches over 2 kilometres in length, comprises a number of open water bodies — the main ones being the Dragonfly Lake and the Kingfisher Lake, and the smaller Water Lily Pond. These are not separate bodies of water but are linked seamlessly to each other, and the water circulates around all the boundaries of the Gardens.

The water in the lakes adds up to about 72,000 cubic metres, or 192 Olympic-sized swimming pools. The bodies of water at Bay South are an integral part of this 54-hectare botanical haven. They enhance the natural environment, sustain an aquatic habitat and create reflecting surfaces. The design of the lake system takes into account aesthetics and hydrology, that is, the movement, quality and distribution of water within the Gardens, especially as the Gardens are located next to the Marina Reservoir catchment area. Marina Reservoir is Singapore's 15th freshwater reservoir, created via a dam called the Marina Barrage and built across the Marina Channel to keep out seawater. Over time and with rainfall, seawater in the reservoir is naturally desalted by rainwater.

Beneath the calm surface of the lakes, an ingenious underwater pumping system is at work. The pumps draw in water from the Marina Channel at the Kingfisher Lake on the southeastern fringe of the Gardens, circulate water through the Gardens in a clockwise direction and discharge water back into the reservoir through the Dragonfly Lake on the northeastern side.

Just as important as the ecological functions of the lakes, the Dragonfly Lake, in particular, forms a second waterfront in the heart of the city centre. Since the Marina Reservoir feeds into Singapore's water supply, water that is collected in the lakes — whether from rainfall or pumped in from Marina Channel — is filtered and cleansed before it is allowed back into the reservoir. Here, both lakes act as an effective natural eco-filter through filter beds that are cleverly incorporated into the waterscape. These comprise aquatic reeds and man-made wetlands lush with aquatic plants, and are located mostly where water enters at the Kingfisher Lake and exits at the Dragonfly Lake. As water passes through the filter beds, the flow is slowed down to give more time for sediments to be filtered out.

Reed beds and constructed islands of aquatic plants also help to maintain water quality by absorbing excess nutrients, particularly nitrogen and phosphorus, which enhance the growth of algae.

The water plants in and around the lakes include water hyacinth and water lettuce, water lilies and mosaic plants, water banana, Nile papyrus, bullrush and hanguana, yellow cabomba, marsh plants such as beach morning glory, Indian shot, barringtonia and ixora, and pandan and Nibung palm on the islands.

Highly visible from the Marina Bay Sands Integrated Resort, the Dragonfly Lake borders, to the north, the future land sale sites that have been reserved for further development such as for boutique hotels and leisure attractions, as part of the building of Singapore's New Downtown around Marina Bay.

With a boardwalk promenade of nearly 500 metres lined with colourful and scented plants, the lake gives visitors a valuable 'windfall' as an urban amenity, another unique place where people can relax in the outdoors in the heart of the financial district, enhancing the quality of life in the surrounding areas as a key aspect in the development of the city centre.

> JUST AS IMPORTANT AS THE ECOLOGICAL FUNCTIONS OF THE LAKES, THE DRAGONFLY LAKE, IN PARTICULAR, FORMS A SECOND WATERFRONT IN THE HEART OF THE CITY CENTRE.

BENEATH THE CALM SURFACE OF THE LAKES, AN INGENIOUS UNDERWATER PUMPING SYSTEM IS AT WORK TO DRAW IN WATER FROM THE MARINA RESERVOIR, CIRCULATE WATER THROUGH THE GARDENS AND DISCHARGE WATER BACK INTO THE RESERVOIR.

Showy and unusual plants at
DRAGONFLY LAKE

Showy

Crinum asiaticum 'Splendens', or red lucky leek

Of the Amaryllidaceae (amaryllis family) and native to tropical and sub-tropical Asia to the Southwestern Pacific and the Mascarene Islands in the Indian Ocean, this herb grows from a subterranean bulb. This cultivar Splendens is a garden selection with showy, deep-red flower buds and petals tinged with red. It is a very effective ornamental plant, and very free-flowering in Singapore, preferring waterlogged or swampy soil. The species is poisonous, but its leaves are used medicinally as a skin treatment to relieve aches, sores and chapped skin, and to treat piles.

Cyperus papyrus, or Nile papyrus

Of the Cyperaceae (sedge family) and native to North Africa, this fast-growing water plant inhabits the edges of lakes and rivers, and may reach up to 4 metres high. The pith of the triangular stems of this plant was used to manufacture the famous scrolls, or papyrus, used by the Egyptians in ancient times, as early as 2,400 BC. Because the written word wielded a power of its own which the Egyptian rulers wanted to keep for themselves, its manufacture was kept as a secret and unfortunately very little evidence remains of this process. Papyrus was later substituted by the Chinese invention of paper made out of plant fibres. Papyrus also had other uses, with its roots used as a source of food, medicine and perfume. The stems were woven into baskets, floor mats, ropes, clothing, footwear and even boats. Today, it is used as a filtering plant, as its roots capture impurities and pollutants, thus lowering the levels of nitrogen in the water.

Typha angustifolia, or bullrush

Of the Typhaceae family and native to the temperate northern hemisphere, the Americas, and places including Nigeria and Kenya, this is a fast-growing, herbaceous aquatic plant reaching 2 metres tall, with stems that grow along the soil surface. It grows at the edges of lakes and rivers, and provides excellent shelter for wild creatures, especially water birds. Its curious inflorescence often figures in cartoons, representing the hiding place of duck hunters. It is one of the main species used to filter and purify the water in the Gardens' lake system.

Red lucky leek

Nile papyrus

Bullrush

Unusual

Typhonodorum lindleyanum, or water banana

Of the Araceae (anthurium family), this aquatic plant is a native of Tanzania and the West Indian Ocean, reaching Madagascar. It is also known as giant aquatic arrowhead, due to the shape of its leaves that point upwards. Its clusters of white flowers open at night and are pollinated by beetles. Its highly poisonous seeds and rootstock are known to be used as famine food on the island of Zanzibar, but they require careful preparation to neutralise the poison they contain.

Hanguana malayana, or Susum

Of the Hanguanaceae family, this is a native of Southeast Asia, and is becoming rare in Singapore, where it is considered vulnerable. It is a rooting aquatic herbaceous plant with strap-shaped leaves and minute flowers, followed by bright red berries. There is some evidence of its use to combat internal parasites.

Leea macrophylla, or *hathikana*

Of the Vitaceae (grape family), this is a native of Southeast Asia, reaching India to the West, where it is known by the Hindi word *hathikana*, meaning 'elephant's ears'. Its large leaves may reach 60 centimetres wide, and the large clusters of tiny cream flowers are quite showy. The medicinal uses of this plant date back to ancient times and are documented in Sanskrit writing. The roots have astringent properties, can be used to kill parasites and pounded to aid the healing of scars.

Water banana

Susum

Hathikana

Recreating Nature

Just as significantly, the Gardens' lake system forms a synergistic link between the western and eastern cores of the Gardens, bringing together the themes in the themed gardens of 'Plants and Planet' in the east and 'Plants and People' in the west. The annotated displays along the lakes depict the role and importance of plants in the healthy functioning of the ecosystem, and further highlight the intimate cultural associations between plants and people and their importance in daily life.

The most important factor is light for plant growth, as this determines the lushness of flowering blooms and foliage, and hence, the amount of floral colour and abundance throughout the Gardens. With the help of a solar insulation map which charts the direction that shadows would fall within the Gardens from the sun, as well as from future adjacent buildings, the designers were able to site the conservatories and the Supertrees in the most optimum locations for plant growth.

To the Gardens' designers, another aspect of equal importance is human comfort, especially in the heat and humidity of Singapore's tropical climate. Comfort is dependent not only on ambient temperatures but also humidity levels. The island's typically high humidity can make for some discomfort, but this can be reduced substantially with a good breeze. Landforms within the Gardens, such as the mounds upon which the themed gardens are presented, turned what was originally a flat space into a three-dimensional landscape, with niches and other new layers of spaces. These landforms are built with the prevailing wind directions in mind, to create spaces whose orientation, shape and alignment invite gentle breezes to blow through. This bit of attention to detail is further enhanced by the judicious placement of shade and shelter, through tree planting, plant trellises and linked canopies, to create an even more conducive environment for exploring the Gardens. For those explorers who would prefer greater speed and comfort, a people-mover system called the Garden Cruiser takes groups of up to 13 around the outdoor gardens in half an hour.

For the main gardens, the project's foreign and local consultants worked together with the Gardens team to adapt the original design intent to local conditions. For example, the height of the landforms had to be moderated, taking into account the large expanse of retaining structural walls that would be required, as well as the need to then green up these walls. The heights of the canopies within the Gardens also had to balance between aesthetics and functionality, in view of Singapore's climate of typical intense rainfall accompanied with winds. Some consultants wanted taller trees, while others advised shorter ones for practical reasons. As the landforms also accommodated the masking of services and amenities such as a food court, design adjustments had to be made to cater to a reduced volume of earth as well as a modified drainage system above these spaces.

Another element of detail is evident in the areas between the four heritage gardens — Indian, Chinese, Malay and Colonial gardens — in the 'Plants and People' section next to the Dragonfly Lake. Like links or stepping-stones, these spaces connect the four gardens. The stories they tell of the interaction between different plants and the various cultures are treated as a type of 'narrative trail', themed tours through the gardens and conservatories that link the different areas via particular topics such as the relationship of plants with food and other aspects of human life and society.

The natural environment created and sustained in the Gardens seeks to replicate Nature not only for the flora but for the fauna as well.

Among the insect species that have come to inhabit the Gardens, the dragonfly is among the most warmly welcomed, for its iconic status as the symbol of the Gardens' corporate logo. Believed to date back 250 million years to the Earth's Permian period, dragonflies are the most visible indicators of water quality and wetland diversity and health — they gather, feed and breed where the water is clean. In this way, they are beautiful and iconic indicators of the health and success of Gardens by the Bay. There are 124 recorded species of dragonfly in Singapore, but some have become extinct because their natural habitat is now harder to find. Some 14 species of dragonfly and four types of damselfly have been sighted at Bay South Garden in surveys leading up to the Gardens' opening in June 2012.

Bird life is another source of fascination for visitors, as the Gardens welcomes feathered visitors, such as kingfishers, herons sunbirds and fishing eagles that have made the Marina Bay and Marina Channel area their new home. Other fauna sighted include monitor lizards, Malaysian box terrapins, red-eared terrapins, tilapia, guppies, mosquito fish and apple snails.

RDENS

[IN THEIR PLANNING OF THE GARDENS AT BAY SOUTH, GRANT ASSOCIATES TOOK INTO ACCOUNT CRITICAL ENVIRONMENTAL FACTORS SUCH AS SOLAR INSULATION, WIND DIRECTIONS AND HUMIDITY LEVELS.

Telling Nature's story

Edutainment is an important aspect in and around the Gardens' lakes and trails. A boardwalk runs alongside the Dragonfly Lake and takes visitors close to the reed beds and filter beds. Interpretive panels, with a narrative trail on the lake system, educate visitors about sustainability and ecology and various other aspects of the Gardens' lake system.

At the central zone of this walk, storyboards and other interpretive media tell how plants clean water in nature and how they provide foraging and roosting habitats for aquatic fauna, as well as the importance of maintaining a healthy aquatic ecosystem in an urban environment. The messages of aquatic ecosystem conservation are also highlighted, together with the cultural associations between some of these plants and people.

These messages of diversity and fragility in the ecosystem are brought to life via a cluster of three man-made 'islands' in the Dragonfly Lake. One depicts models of the native mangrove tree species and other plants that once dominated Singapore's coastal habitat. The two other islands are planted with native coastal vegetation, such as the breadnut, Kelumpang and octopus tree (*Schefflera actinophylla*). These plants have been used extensively by the local people for fuel, food, housing and boat-making, but are becoming scarce in Singapore and Southeast Asia today.

The displays also tell the story behind why and how the lake system was planned and constructed, and explain the role of water in nourishing forests and how nature works to refresh and renew itself — with some help from man, as in these gardens. Overall, an important aim is to show the significance of clean water to man and the biodiversity that becomes possible because of it, as the Gardens themselves demonstrate.

The islands and walks surrounding the Dragonfly Lake are planted with native plants from Singapore's coastal habitats. At the Scented Walk, a sensorial experience of fragrance and colour awaits, where the freshwater mangrove (*Barringtonia acutangula*) and the red pong pong tree (*Cerbera manghas* cv.) provide a foil for different cultivars of mussaenda (*Mussaenda* 'Queen Sirikit', *Mussaenda phillippica* 'Aurorae'), pigeon berry (*Duranta repens*) and Buah Karang Utan (*Tarenna odorata*), amongst many others.

Strategically placed in the inaccessible islands, the well-established populations of Nibung palm (*Oncosperma tigillarium*), screwpine (*Pandanus tectorius*) and octopus tree harbour birds such as the small crane, kingfishers and golden orioles.

Buah Karang Utan

Mussaenda 'Queen Sirikit'

Red pong pong tree

Mussaenda philippica 'Aurorae'

[THE MESSAGES OF DIVERSITY AND FRAGILITY IN THE ECOSYSTEM ARE BROUGHT TO LIFE VIA A CLUSTER OF THREE MAN-MADE 'ISLANDS' IN THE DRAGONFLY LAKE.

A wonderland by night.
When evening falls,
the serene nature of
the whole site is at its
most inviting.

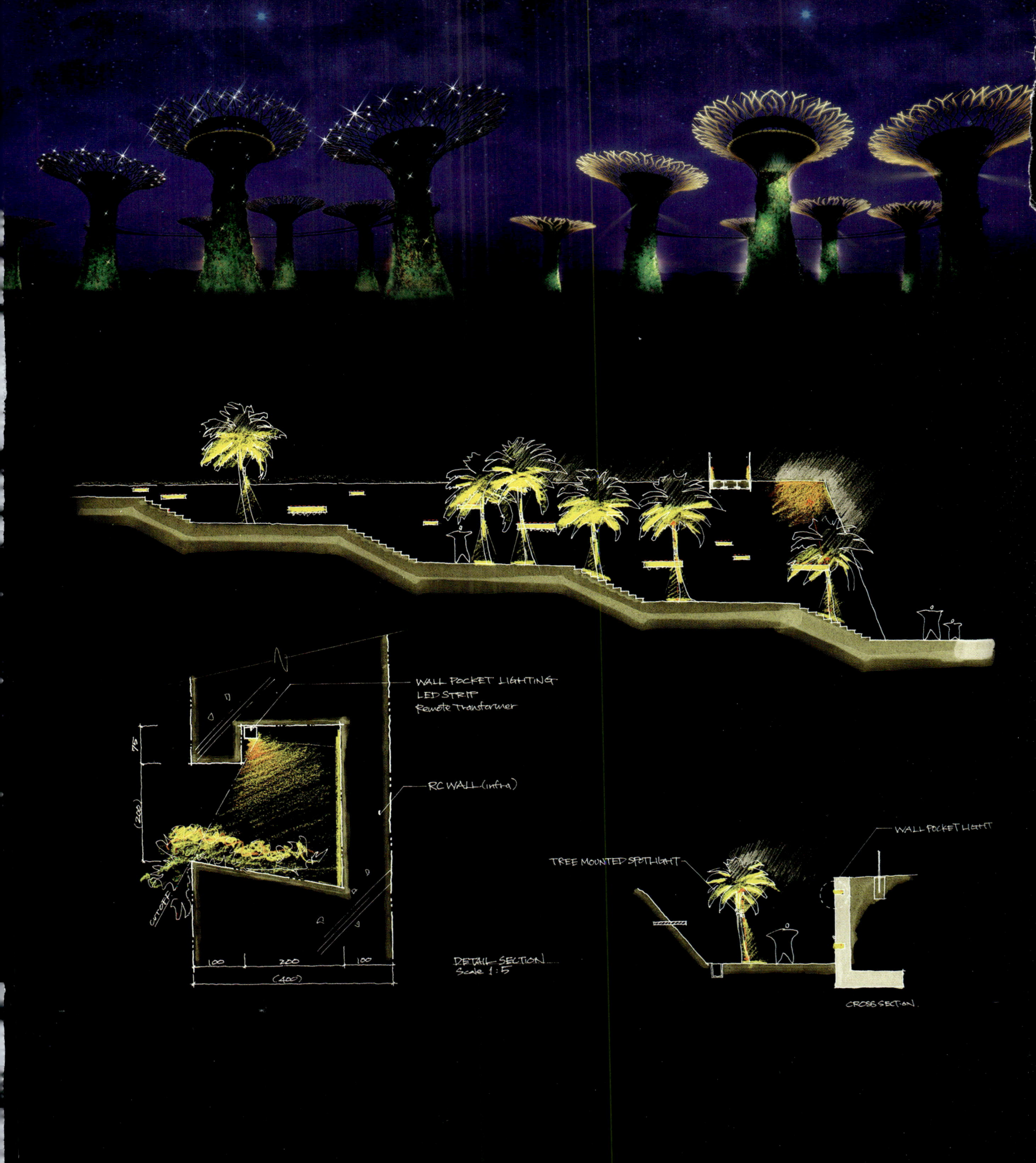

A wonderland by night

Nightfall brings added splendour to Gardens by the Bay, as a garden whose setting surrounded by water creates opportunity for especially inviting imagery through reflection and other lighting effects. The nocturnal wonderland of clusters of coloured and moving lights beckons to visitors from nearby vantage points such as the SkyPark of the Marina Bay Sands resort and along the East Coast Parkway.

The nighttime splendour of Gardens by the Bay is designed and developed by Lighting Planners Associates, a Tokyo-based firm that has worked on other lighting projects in Singapore. The design concept can be summed up as 'Entertainment with Organic Lighting'. The lighting scheme is intended to be natural as well as entertaining, in an ongoing 'dialogue' with the foliage and water. This is achieved in several ways — by creating artistic combinations of light and shadow; having soothing interactive lighting to engage visitors by helping to convey the communicative power of trees, water, wind and other natural elements; and creating spaces to facilitate the discovery of 'spiritual forces' inside the tree groves. All these create effects of mystery and interactivity. The key is not to light up everything, but to play with focus and fantasy, shadow and suggestion.

As visitors wander through the Gardens after dusk, they discover various special aspects of lighting. For example, at the Fragile Forest, it will seem as if fireflies are congregating along the water's edge, while some kind of mysterious light seems to waver in the breeze and in the deep darkness of the tree groves. Various techniques and devices such as motion sensors and those that create shadows are employed to complement and enhance the lighting schemes.

Underpinning the display of light and mystery is adherence to a key design principle of creating 'comfortable shadows', where light and shadow are carefully positioned amongst the plants, to make for a beautiful contrast for a rhythmical nightscape. Light fixtures that are fundamentally for nighttime are well-concealed and integrated into the environment, thereby minimising potential glare and harshness at night and blending well with the landscape during the day. A careful balance of 'vertical luminescence' enhances visitors' appreciation of the Gardens' nocturnal environment. Higher vertical luminescence in many spaces throughout the Gardens is used effectively, for instance, at outdoor walls or in up-lights on trees and foliage.

The dynamism of the Gardens in the nighttime is maintained while also observing sustainability concerns of energy consumption. Energy conservation measures include using high-efficiency light sources and fixtures, light sensors and dimming control systems. A measure of self-sufficiency in lighting is provided by seven of the Supertrees that are equipped with photovoltaic features such as solar panels that power some 67 per cent of the energy required to light the Supertrees at night.

These complementary aspects are part of the overall aim to evoke a sense of garden artistry in various ways, down to the careful selection of every plant according to species, size and maturity, and interesting form, as well as their subsequent meticulous positioning.

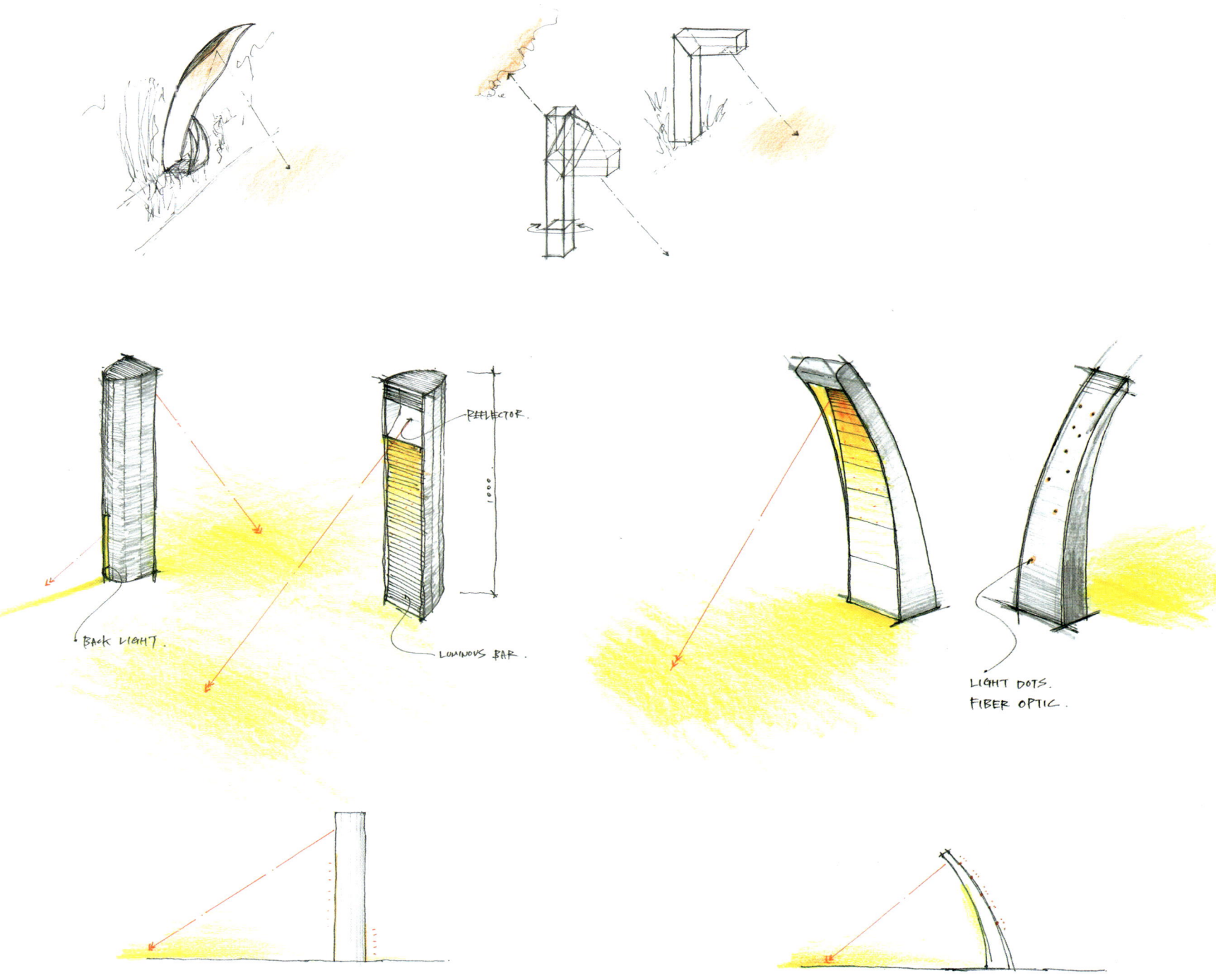

7
A New Future of Perpetual Spring

As it takes shape and takes its place in Singapore's new downtown around Marina Bay, Gardens by the Bay will transform Singapore even more.

WHEN GARDENS BY THE BAY TAKES ITS PLACE IN SINGAPORE'S NEW DOWNTOWN IN MARINA BAY, THESE WATERFRONT GARDENS WILL UNDERPIN THE TRANSFORMATION OF SINGAPORE FROM A GARDEN CITY INTO A TROPICAL CITY IN A GARDEN. INSTEAD OF HAVING A HOME DECORATED WITH A GARDEN, WE HAVE NOW SET THE HOME WITHIN THE GARDEN ITSELF.

MRS THERESA FOO

Chairman of Gardens by the Bay, which was incorporated as a company limited by guarantee in November 2011 to manage the operations of the gardens and serve national and public interests.

> ALREADY A SOURCE OF NATIONAL PRIDE FOR SINGAPOREANS, THE GARDENS WILL POSITION SINGAPORE AS A DISTINCTIVE GLOBAL CITY AND PREMIER LEISURE DESTINATION FOR PEOPLE AROUND THE WORLD.

The surrounding green ambience will sustain a unique environment for people to live, work and play, all within a dynamic city centre day and night. This will be a key emblem of Singapore's City in a Garden vision, based on the idea that Singapore is developing far beyond its longstanding Garden City roots by now nurturing the whole country as one big garden.

The completion of the first phase of the 54-hectare Bay South Garden marks the foundation phase of the Gardens by the Bay. Together with Bay East Garden and Bay Central Garden at 32 and 15 hectares respectively, the three interconnected waterfront gardens will eventually fan out around Marina Bay, each with its own distinctive design and character.

At the Bay South Garden, carefully selected and nurtured plants from around the world bring to life and encapsulate the themes of 'Plants and Planet' and 'Plants and People'. The messages of sustainability and biodiversity are presented through dynamic plant displays and interpretive media in various features within the Gardens, including the two cooled conservatories, Supertrees, themed gardens and the gardens around the Dragonfly and Kingfisher Lakes. The main platforms for further development and promotion of these themes are three key events spaces — the Flower Field and Function Space within the Flower Dome cool-dry conservatory, the Supertree Grove at the heart of Bay South Garden surrounded by the themed gardens, and The Meadow to the west of the Gardens beside the Dragonfly Lake.

These spaces give added character to different parts of the Gardens. The Meadow, where the 'concert bowl' is, has a capacity of 30,000 people and can accommodate mass audience events such as musical concerts. It is Singapore's largest outdoor garden event venue, with a stunning backdrop view of the conservatories, Supertrees and cityscape.

The Silver Leaf, an area under a cluster of silver-themed Supertrees and overlooking the Dragonfly Lake with a good view of the Marina Bay skyline, is well-suited to quieter events such as weddings and anniversaries. The Lily Pad, overlooking the Kingfisher Lake and next to a children's playground called the Tadpole Play Area, caters to more active occasions such as children's parties. The Supertree Grove, under the shelter of the Gardens' main cluster of Supertrees is a perfect venue for corporate events such as product launches, especially at night when the surrounding themed gardens are enhanced with lighting effects.

Visitors to Bay South will enjoy an excellent experience through programmes that highlight the characteristics and features of the Gardens and which cater to all in the community. Overall, programming at Gardens by the Bay focuses on providing edutainment within a unique garden setting, to entertain visitors while fostering an appreciation of plants and the environment, and their relationship to man.

The Gardens will be a prime leisure attraction with a host of events and activities to actively engage the public. The distinctive themed gardens, conservatories and informative trails — as well as the changing floral displays — will also help promote a new way of looking at plants. The leisure programme focuses on generating buzz at the Gardens with inclusive and accessible programmes that reach out to different audience segments. These include shows and performances for the general public, as well as more customised community, arts and educational programmes curated around a common theme. These will take the form of signature events that the public can identify the Gardens with (such as the Supertree Light and Sound Show, concerts at The Meadow, and other lifestyle events and performances) or programmes put together in collaboration with partners such as grassroots associations, performance arts groups and sponsors.

Food and beverage amenities, some of them botanically-themed, will also be well-integrated into the development of the Gardens. The Bay South Garden opened in June 2012 with some 13 food and beverage spaces spread across the gardens. These spaces cater to the whole spectrum of taste, ranging from the local heritage outlet Satay by the Bay to trendy international cuisine, and will be further expanded and refined as the Gardens are more fully developed.

Different thematic threads will unify the changing displays and the leisure programmes for an immersive experience throughout the year. For instance, 2012 will be the year of 'Celebrating Festivities', and the calendar of events includes floral displays that relate plants to festivities, with events and activities linked to

> OVERALL, PROGRAMMING AT GARDENS BY THE BAY FOCUSES ON PROVIDING EDUTAINMENT WITHIN A UNIQUE GARDEN SETTING, TO ENTERTAIN VISITORS WHILE FOSTERING AN APPRECIATION OF PLANTS AND THE ENVIRONMENT, AND THEIR RELATIONSHIP TO MAN.

festivals commonly celebrated in Singapore as well as throughout the world. These could be universal celebrations such as New Year's Eve, Christmas, Valentine's Day and Mother's Day, or themed around topics such as the environment (for example, World Environment Day and Earth Day). More Singapore-centred occasions include National Day as well as events geared towards education and community bonding, and the arts, food, sports and fashion. Some of these, when proven successful in the Gardens' context and with particular appeal to visitors, may evolve into signature events over time.

The approach of 'edutainment' denotes catering to recreation with an underlying educational component, to bring about a deeper and broader appreciation of plants, nature and the environment, especially for younger visitors. Educational elements are introduced in the Gardens through the annotations accompanying the displays and along the trails, as well as the interpretive media, exhibits and publications. Beyond this, guided tours, talks, workshops and exhibitions provide an enriching edutainment experience for all visitors to the Gardens. Some of these aspects — such as the Heritage Gardens which depict the use of plants by the different cultures in Singapore, and the World of Plants which showcase botany in an outdoor classroom setting — can bring to life what is learnt in the school curriculum.

Visitors who wish to participate in the making of the Gardens can join the Gardens' Friends and Volunteer programme to help in the areas of programming, horticulture and operations.

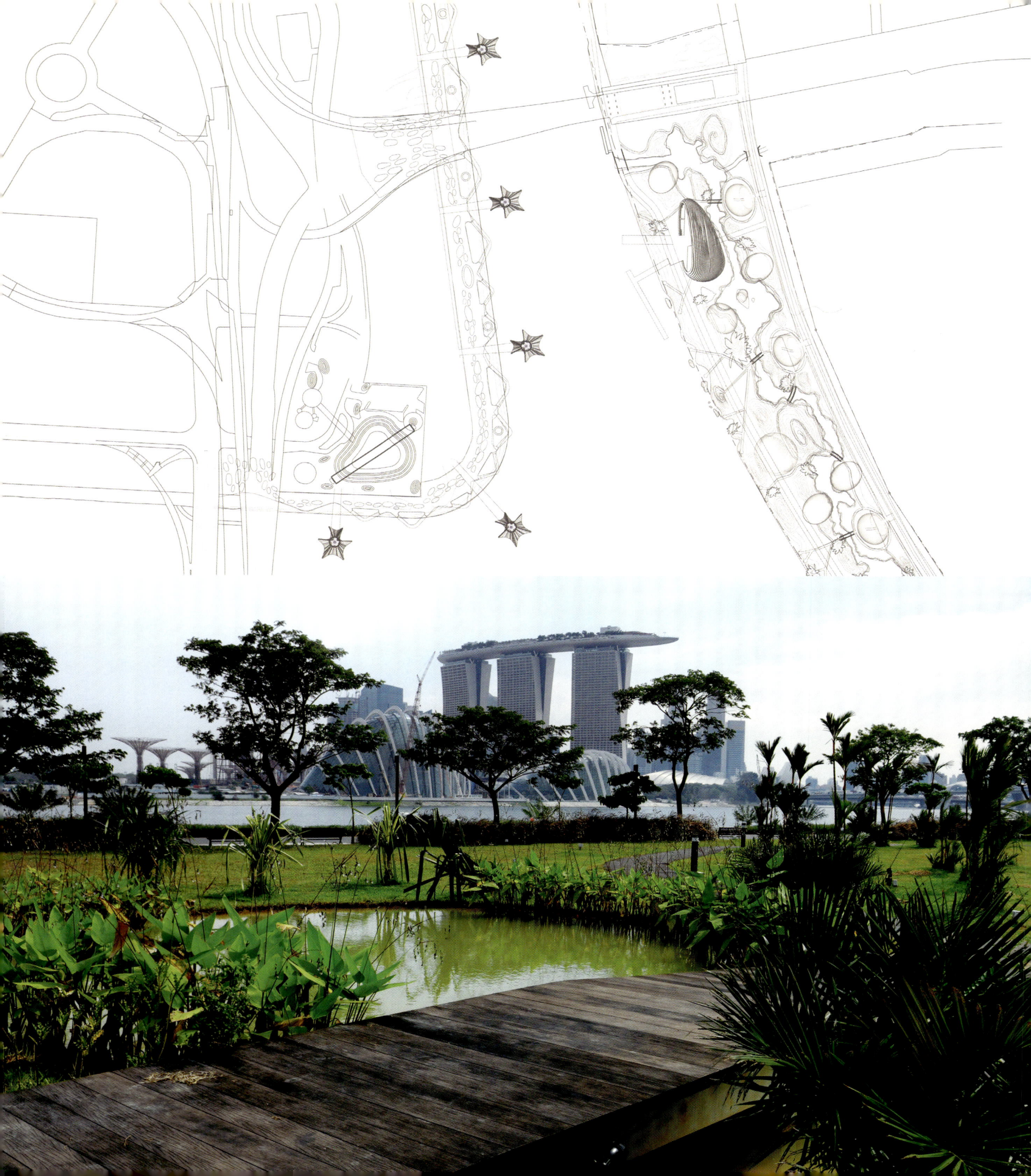

TWO MORE GARDENS
Bay East and Bay Central

The official opening in June 2012 of Bay South Garden of Gardens by the Bay marks the start of a phased opening. Eventually, all 101 hectares of all three gardens will be completed at some stage after 2012.

Phase Two of Bay South's development will include attractions such as a main event space and the Flower Market, which will later become the main entry precinct into the Gardens.

After Bay South, the next to be developed will be the Bay East Garden, directly opposite to the east of Bay South across the Marina Channel, linked by a pathway on foot traversing Marina Barrage. The Bay East Garden was used as a staging site for the rowing and canoeing events of the inaugural Youth Olympic Games hosted by Singapore in August 2010. Thereafter, reinstatement works were carried out and completed in September 2011. In November 2011, it was opened as an interim public garden, with a promenade and visitor facilities in place.

The implementation of the masterplan for Bay East Garden — designed by American landscape architect Kathryn Gustafson and her London-based design firm Gustafson Porter — will be carried out at a later stage, taking into consideration the surrounding infrastructural works in the vicinity. The gardens' 2-kilometre promenade will host a series of tropical leaf-shaped gardens. Five water inlets will be aligned with the prevailing wind direction, thus maximising and extending the shoreline while allowing wind and water to penetrate the site to help cool areas of activity around them. These spaces will enable visitors to enjoy serene garden experiences while looking westward at the Bay South Garden, as the conservatories are reflected in the waters of the Marina Reservoir, and with the entire financial district and Marina Bay as a backdrop.

At a later stage, the 15-hectare Bay Central Garden will be built, with waterfront attractions linking Bay South and Bay East along a 3-kilometre promenade. This third garden will eventually realise its own masterplan that began to be developed in 2012.

Acknowledgements

Perpetual Spring: Singapore's Gardens by the Bay has been almost four years in the making, from 2008. Along the way, the final fruit of this publication has ripened from constant fertilisation and careful tending, through numerous site visits and interviews, and pruning from rich materials.

The many people to be thanked include the following:

GARDENS BY THE BAY

- **Dr Kiat W Tan** *Chief Executive Officer*
- **Kenneth Er** *Chief Operating Officer*
- **Ng Boon Gee** *Assistant Director, Gardens Operations*
- **Andy Kwek** *Assistant Director, Conservatory Operations*
- **Anton van der Schans** *Assistant Director, Horticulture*
- **Harry Luther** *Assistant Director, Research*
- **Christopher Dalzell** *Section Head, Friends and Volunteers*
- **Daniela Cristina Zappi** *Senior Researcher*
- **Derek Chan** *Senior Landscape Architect*
- **Andrea Kee** *Section Head, Gardens Horticulture*
- **Richard Pang** *Assistant Director, Facilities*
- **Felicia Chua** *Manager, Nursery*
- **Lim Mei Leng** *Manager, Horticulture*
- **Melissa Tan** *Manager, Horticulture*
- **Janice Loh** *Manager, Gardens Operations*
- **Patrick Hayes** *Manager, Horticulture Conservatory*
- **Sean Koh** *Manager, Floriculture*
- **Arthur Voo** *Officer, Research*
- **Chong Jia Zhen** *Officer, Horticulture*
- **Melissa Wong** *Officer, Horticulture*
- **Lee Xiaoyi** *Officer, Horticulture*
- **Ng Wing Fatt** *Officer, Horticulture*
- **Ong Chui Leng** *Deputy Director, Programming*
- **Prisca Teh** *Assistant Director, Retail*
- **Michelle Lim** *Assistant Director, Public Relations*
- **Ong Yan Szu** *Section Head, Corporate Communications and Publication*
- **Aisyah Rahim** *Executive, Corporate Communications*

GRANT ASSOCIATES

Andrew Grant *Project Director (Landscape)*

WILKINSON EYRE ARCHITECTS

Paul Baker *Director (Architect)*
Matthew Potter *Project Architect*

ATELIER ONE

Neil Thomas *Director*

ATELIER TEN

Patrick Bellows *Director (Environmental Engineering)*

LIGHTING PLANNERS ASSOCIATES INC

Kaoru Mende *Principal*
Reiko Kasai *Director (Singapore Branch)*

PM LINK

Ong Pang Wee, Max *Senior Project Manager*

PHOTOGRAPHS

Andy Kwek
Daniela Cristina Zappi
Heng Photoshop
Ho Kun Hee (Kunst Photography)
Kenneth Er
Munshi Ahmed
Quek-Phua Lek Kheng, Jassy

DRAWINGS AND IMAGES

Grant Associates
Lighting Planners Associates Inc
Wilkinson Eyre Architects

For their significant contributions to this book:

THE AUTHOR WOULD LIKE TO THANK

Dr Kiat W Tan *for information on the genesis of Gardens by the Bay*

Kenneth Er *for technical information on the cooling system of the conservatories and lake system*

Daniela Zappi *for vetting the drafts and information on the plants*

Harry Luther *for information on plants, particularly bromeliads*

Aisyah Rahim *for assistance with getting the photographs*

Ong Yan Szu *for facilitating early research, arranging interviews and photoshoots, reading the drafts and providing all manner of help necessary for this publication*

ABOUT THE AUTHOR

Koh Buck Song is a Singaporean writer and consultant in branding, communications and corporate social responsibility. This is his 21st book as author and editor. His other books include *Brand Singapore: How Nation Branding Built Asia's Leading Global City* (2011) and *Brighter: Electricity In Singapore: From Beginning To Beyond* (2011).

Consultants and Main Contractors of the Gardens by the Bay Project:

PROJECT MANAGEMENT

PM Link Pte Ltd

CONSULTANTS

Atelier One *Structural Engineers*

Atelier Ten *Mechanical & Electrical Engineers*

CPG Consultants Pte Ltd *Architectural, Mechanical & Electrical Engineers, Civil & Structural Engineers, and Quantity Surveyors*

Davis Langdon & Seah *Quantity Surveyor (Singapore Office)*

Grant Associates *Masterplanner*

Land Design Studio *Interpretative Consultants*

Meinhardt Infrastructure Pte Ltd *Civil & Structural Engineers*

Wilkinson Eyre Architects *Architect*

MAIN CONTRACTORS

Expand Construction Pte Ltd

Koon Construction & Transport Co. Pte Ltd

Planar One & Associates Pte Ltd

Precise Development Pte Ltd

Swee Hong Engineering Construction Pte Ltd

Woh Hup Pte Ltd

© 2012 National Parks Board

Perpetual Spring – Singapore's Gardens by the Bay

Project Editor   : Lee Mei Lin
Project Designer : Lynn Chin Nyuk Ling

All photographs and illustrations courtesy of Gardens by the Bay

Published in 2012 by Marshall Cavendish Editions
An imprint of Marshall Cavendish International
1 New Industrial Road
Singapore 536196
Tel: (65) 6213 9300 Fax: (65) 6285 4871
E-mail: genrefsales@sg.marshallcavendish.com
Website: www.marshallcavendish.com/genref

All rights reserved. No part of this publication may be reproduced, stored in a retrieval system
or transmitted, in any form or by any means, electronic, mechanical, photocopying, recording or
otherwise, without the prior permission of the copyright owner. Requests for permission should
be addressed to the Publisher.

Other Marshall Cavendish Offices
Marshall Cavendish Corporation. 99 White Plains Road, Tarrytown NY 10591-9001, USA • Marshall Cavendish International (Thailand) Co Ltd. 253 Asoke, 12th Flr, Sukhumvit 21 Road, Klongtoey Nua, Wattana, Bangkok 10110, Thailand • Marshall Cavendish (Malaysia) Sdn Bhd, Times Subang, Lot 46, Subang Hi-Tech Industrial Park, Batu Tiga, 40000 Shah Alam, Selangor Darul Ehsan, Malaysia

Marshall Cavendish is a trademark of Times Publishing Limited

National Library Board, Singapore Cataloguing-in-Publication Data
Koh, Buck Song.
Perpetual spring, Singapore's Gardens by the Bay / Koh Buck Song. – Singapore :
Marshall Cavendish Editions, 2012.
p. cm.

ISBN : 978-981-4398-18-3
ISBN : 978-981-2618-47-4 (pbk.)

1. Urban gardens – Singapore. 2. Gardens – Singapore. I. Title.

SB470.55
712.5095957 -- dc23   OCN781609432

Printed on recycled paper by Saik Wah Print Media Pte Ltd